CÔTE D'IVOIRE

Patricia Sheehan

MARSHALL CAVENDISH
New York • London • Sydney

Reference edition reprinted 2001 by
Marshall Cavendish Corporation
99 White Plains Road
Tarrytown
New York 10591

© Times Media Private Limited 2000

Originated and designed by
Times Books International, an imprint of
Times Media Private Limited, a member of the
Times Publishing Group

Printed in Malaysia

Library of Congress Cataloging-in-Publication Data:

Sheehan, Patricia, 1954–
     Côte d'Ivoire = Ivory Coast / Patricia Sheehan.
         p. cm.—(Cultures of the World)
     Includes bibliographical references (p.) and index.
     Summary: Surveys the geography, history, government,
economy, and culture of Côte d'Ivoire, formerly known as the
Ivory Coast.
     ISBN 0-7614-0980-7 (lib. bdg.)
     1. Côte d'Ivoire—Juvenile literature. [1. Côte d'Ivoire.]
I. Title. II. Title: Ivory Coast. III. Series.
DT545.22.S54   2000
966.68—dc21   99-27250
                      CIP
                      AC

INTRODUCTION

THE RÉPUBLIQUE DE CÔTE D'IVOIRE, formerly known as the Ivory Coast, was given its name in the 14th century by French sailors who traded ivory there. The area became a French colony in 1893. It only gained independence in 1960.

Independence brought about many challenges to this young West African state—the creation of a nation, the introduction of a multiparty democratic government, adequate education and healthcare for its people, and coping with high population growth rates and environmental and social issues.

Côte d'Ivoire has an economy that is largely dependent on agriculture and the cocoa industry. It is the world's leading producer of cocoa. Its greatest resource is its multi-ethnic people, who live together in harmony. When political and social conflicts arise, they are addressed through discussion, not violence or military intervention. This is a cause for optimism and confidence in the future of Côte d'Ivoire.

CONTENTS

This is not some exotic tree growth but an ingenious way of storing corncobs out of harm's way.

CONTENTS

A warrior mask. Its purpose is to maintain order within a tribe.

GEOGRAPHY

CÔTE D'IVOIRE ("coht dee-voh-AH") IS SITUATED on the west coast of Africa. With an area of 124,470 square miles (322,460 square km), slightly larger than the state of New Mexico, the country shares its borders with Mali and Burkina Faso in the north, Liberia and Guinea on the west, and Ghana on the east. To the south is the Gulf of Guinea, and beyond it the Atlantic Ocean. The country's topography consists of coastal lowland, rainforest plateau, and upland savanna.

LANDSCAPES

In the south of Côte d'Ivoire is a 320-mile (515-km) wide strip of coastal land on the Gulf of Guinea. This area is marked by a number of lagoons and sandy beaches.

The southeast and central regions are home to the Baule, Agni, and Abron peoples. The land around their farms contains the remnants of

Left: **As more forests are cut down to make room for modern developments, the natural habitat for elephants and other wildlife has decreased significantly.**

Opposite: **Abidjan is the largest port in French-speaking Africa.**

7

rainforests that once covered the entire southern Côte d'Ivoire. Since 1975, the country has had the highest rate of deforestation in the world. The remaining rainforest extends about 60 miles (97 km) in from the coast to the central region and about 165 miles (265 km) from east to west.

In the north, the land changes to savanna. Compared to many parts of Africa, the arable land is mostly flat with relatively rich, sandy soil. Such terrain favors the growing of crops, mainly dry rice, peanuts, and millet.

In the northwest are two mountainous regions, called the Odienné and Man, where several summits rise to more than 5,000 feet (1,524 m). The highest peak, Mount Nimba, towers at 5,750 feet (1,752 m).

RIVERS

The principal rivers are the Sassandra, Bandama, and Komoé. Each river is only navigable for about 40 miles (64 km) of its total length because during the dry season, the water levels are extremely low, and during the rainy season, it is nearly impossible to navigate through the rapids.

MAIN NATIONAL PARKS

KOMOÉ NATIONAL PARK, about 350 miles (563 km) from the city of Abidjan, is West Africa's largest game park. Tucked in the northeast corner of Côte d'Ivoire, it has an area of about 4,440 square miles (11,500 square km). One of the most popular hunting tracks during the dry season is along the Komoé River, where most of the game comes in search of water. Animals found in the Komoé park include elephants, lions, hippopotamus, leopards, antelopes, colobus and green monkeys, and wild hogs. Over 400 species of birds can be spotted.

TAÏ NATIONAL PARK is one of the last remaining virgin rainforests in West Africa. It is about 1,400 square miles (3,626 square km). Trees extend up to 165 feet (50 m), with massive trunks and huge supporting roots. This primary forest consists of monumental trees, hanging tropical plants called lianas, torrential streams, and resident wildlife.

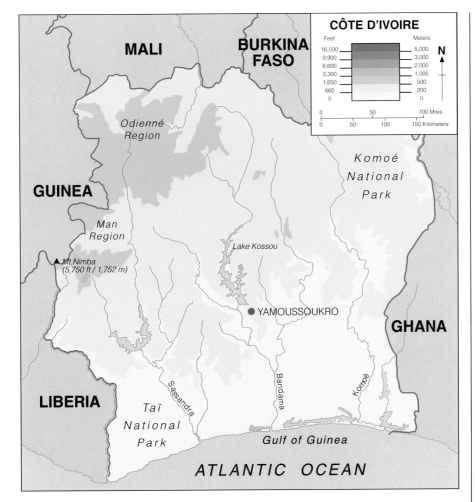

The country has three seasons—November to March is warm and dry; March to May is hot and dry; June to October is hot and wet. July is the wettest of all months.

CLIMATE

Côte d'Ivoire has two distinct climatic zones. Along the coast, the weather is humid. Temperatures vary from 70°F (21°C) to 90°F (32°C). In the northern savanna, temperature differences are more extreme. In the summer, temperatures can drop to 54°F (12°C) at night and rise above 104°F (40°C) in the day. The northern area has an average annual rainfall of 55 inches (140 cm), while annual rainfall in the southern region is 60 to 80 inches (152 to 203 cm). From early December to February, strong harmattan winds blow sand from the Sahara, reducing visibility in the northern mountain regions.

Above: **A baobab tree.**

Right: **Birds along a river in the savanna.**

FLORA

The savanna is covered by low grasses, shrubs, and small deciduous trees. In this arid zone the unusual baobab tree survives by storing water in its trunk, which allows it to get through the dry season. The trunk of the baobab tree can grow to a diameter of 26 feet (8 m). In times of drought, elephants will break into the trunk to get at its water.

Central and southern Côte d'Ivoire is covered by forests with more than 225 species of trees. This area of tropical rainforest receives an average annual rainfall of more than 50 inches (127 cm). Evergreens and oil palms tower above its dense surface covering of shrubs, ferns, and mosses. There are numerous species of tropical hardwood trees, including obeche, mahogany, and iroko (African teak). This area is a great natural resource, because tropical hardwoods are commercially valuable.

RAINFOREST DESTRUCTION

With the Taï National Park the only remaining virgin forest in Côte d'Ivoire, rainforest destruction and the consequent damage to the environment is now of national concern. In only 10 years, from 1977 to 1987, 42% of the rainforest was lost. Neighboring Ghana only lost 8%. The estimate is that within 40 years, the country's forests will be gone.

Deforestation has increased over the years because of the expansion of the timber industry and agriculture. When coffee and cocoa prices fell in the 1980s, the country concentrated on exporting wood to Europe, its largest trading partner. The timber industry exports the same amount of hardwood per year as Brazil, a country 20 times larger than Côte d'Ivoire. Every day ships in the port of Abidjan are loaded with logs. Millions of acres of tropical rainforest have also been destroyed to make room for cocoa and other commodity plantations. Since cocoa trees deplete the soil's nutrients very quickly, plantation owners have to constantly clear virgin forest to take advantage of its fertile soil.

Subsistence farming methods practiced by small-scale farmers greatly increase the rate of deforestation. Destructive forest fires occur regularly because extensive slash-and-burn practices leave too many openings in the forest cover.

In order to transport timber from the forests and agricultural produce from the plantations, more roads were built. This has destroyed many natural habitats, endangering the native animals. When people's source of food is depleted, they are forced to move.

The results of deforestation are the extinction of plants and animals, the loss of medicinal plants, as well as an increase in malaria, changes in rainfall patterns leading to infertile land, and radically altered rural living conditions.

FAUNA

The animal life in Côte d'Ivoire is similar to that of its neighbor Ghana. Characterized by a great variety of distinctive animals and birds, the country's wildlife is part of the Ethiopian biogeographic zone. Herds of elephants roam the woodlands and grasslands, which are also home to the chimpanzees. Carnivores, such as hyenas, jackals, and panthers, live in the same region. There are a large number of antelope and wild hogs in the country; the most plentiful hog is the red river hog. Manatees, or herbivorous water animals, also live in some rivers. The Taï National Park is notable for its pygmy hippopotamuses.

Most bird life belongs to Eurasian groups. The guinea fowl is the main game bird. It lives in the forests and is covered with bluish-white spots, and has a red throat and a crest of curly black feathers. In the savanna the blue-bellied roller bird, which has a green beak and feet, is common. The birds are easily spotted on bushes where they look for insects.

Reptiles found in the country include lizards and crocodiles. Pythons and a variety of venomous snakes can also be found. There are many insects, notably mosquitoes, driver ants, termites, locusts, and tsetse flies.

PRINCIPAL CITIES

YAMOUSSOUKRO, with a population of 150,000, is also called the "Radiant City." Yamoussoukro is easily accessible from all parts of the country because of its central location. In 1983 it was designated the official capital by former President Félix Houphouët-Boigny. The highways in the city are lined with over 10,000 street lights, but there are few cars. The city's economy is primarily dependent on the timber and perfume industries, and the country's major export crops, cocoa and coffee, are grown here. Despite the influence of Houphouët-Boigny, a complete transfer of government offices from Abidjan, the old colonial capital, has never really occurred.

Below: **A woman hurries to the market with her load while farmers till the land.**

Opposite: **Many animals live along the Komoé River, including antelopes.**

Above: The name Abidjan is the result of a misunderstanding. After landing at Abidjan, some French soldiers asked a local resident what place it was. He thought they had asked why he was there, so he replied in the Ebrié language, "T'chan m'bi jan," which means, "I've returned to cut some leaves." The soldiers, refusing to admit that they did not understand him, reported back that the place was called Abidjan.

Opposite: Bouaké is home to the country's largest and oldest textile factory.

ABIDJAN was a small fishing village of about 700 inhabitants when it became the terminus of the railroad to the interior in 1904. Nevertheless, with no port facilities, growth was slow. In 1934, when Côte d'Ivoire was still a French colony, Abidjan became the capital. It retained this status even after independence because by then, the French had finished building the Vridi canal, which connected Abidjan's lagoon to the ocean. This instantly gave the city an excellent harbor, and modern port operations commenced soon after. Today, Abidjan is Côte d'Ivoire's main port and largest city.

Over the years, the population of Abidjan has skyrocketed to almost three million people, spread over four peninsulas around the lagoon. Known as the "Paris of West Africa," Abidjan has a large French population. It also attracts Africans from neighboring countries, making it the region's most cosmopolitan city.

Abidjan is the hub of the country's rail and road system and the center of its cultural and commercial life. Many government offices have remained there. It is home to the national university, several technical colleges, libraries, and an art museum. The city is attractive and modern with many parks and wide boulevards, a legacy from the French. Since the late 1980s, Abidjan has had one of the worst reputations for crime in West Africa, making it unsafe to wander around alone after dark.

BOUAKÉ is located in central Côte d'Ivoire, where the southern forests meet the savanna. It is the second largest city, with over 800,000 residents. Bouaké was established as a French military post in the late 1890s and once served as an important slave market. It is now an important administrative and commercial center. In addition, it is the central market for cocoa, coffee, cotton, yams, and other products produced in the region. Bouaké is also the site of a school of forestry and a cotton-textile research institute.

Other urban centers include Man in the west, Korhogo in the north, Bondoukou in the east, and San-Pédro in the south. San-Pédro is the second major port and is a center for the export of timber and palm oil.

HISTORY

INDEPENDENT TRIBAL KINGDOMS flourished in Côte d'Ivoire for many centuries before the Europeans became interested in exploring the African continent. Unfortunately, very little is known about these kingdoms prior to the arrival of European ships in the 1460s. What is clear, however, is that from as early as the 8th century A.D., Côte d'Ivoire was an important center for many trade routes that spread north across the Sahara. Traders exchanged gold, kola nuts, and slaves for cloth, utensils, and salt.

EUROPEANS AND THE SLAVE TRADE

The first sustained European interest in Africa developed in the late 15th century under the tutelage of the Prince of Portugal. The Portuguese were motivated by a variety of impulses—a desire for knowledge, a wish to bring Christianity to the pagan peoples, the search for potential allies against the Muslims, and the hope of finding slaves and new trade routes.

Opposite: **After the Europeans arrived in Côte d'Ivoire, the ivory trade thrived. However, since 1997, with increased ivory smuggling, there has been a ban in the country in the trade of elephant tusks in order to protect the national symbol, the elephant.**

Left: **With a rise in demand for slaves in the United States for plantation work, millions of Africans became victims. Most were captured by other Africans and exchanged for various consumer goods.**

17

The Europeans were attracted to the country not only because of the ivory trade, but also because there was a huge supply of African slaves.

The Portuguese established a chain of trading settlements along the West African coast. African gold, ivory, foodstuffs, and slaves were exchanged for ironware, firearms, textiles, and foodstuffs. The new trade had radical effects. Previous trade routes had been via the Sahara. When it was redirected to the coast, battles soon broke out among the coastal people for control over trade and access to firearms from Europe. The situation also attracted other Europeans who, throughout the 16th century, attempted to control the existing trade.

Fortunately for the inhabitants of Côte d'Ivoire, European slaving and merchant ships preferred other areas along the coast, such as Sierra Leone and Ghana, as they had better harbors. So the nation did not suffer.

During the late 18th century, after years of profiting from the slave trade, Great Britain decided to abolish it. Their decision led to increased Christian missionary activity in the region. Following on the heels of the missionaries came the European explorers, and this exploration stimulated the interest of merchants searching for new markets.

FRENCH TAKEOVER

In the late 18th century, French merchants became interested in Côte d'Ivoire, and so did their government, but it was not until the 19th century that France began to exploit opportunities in the country. In the 1840s the French government enticed local chiefs with gifts and money to grant French commercial traders a monopoly along the coast in exchange for an annual rent and French protection.

The French then built naval bases to keep out other traders. After signing treaties with coastal rulers, they moved inland to begin a systematic conquest of the interior. There they met fierce guerrilla resistance and became embroiled in a long war.

Opposite: **A former colonial resort in Grand Bassam.**

Côte d'Ivoire became a French colony in 1893 and part of French West Africa by 1904. Fierce resistance by the guerrillas, which included the Baule and other eastern tribal groups, continued until 1918. Faced with such resistance, the French became increasingly authoritarian in their efforts to retain power.

The French had one goal—to stimulate the production of exports. They planted coffee, cocoa, and oil palms along the coast, and changed existing patterns of trade and political, economic, and religious systems. They built transportation systems so that raw materials could be shipped easily to ports for export. Tax systems were instituted, forcing subsistence farmers to increase the production of cash crops or engage in migrant labor.

Côte d'Ivoire stood out as the only West African country with a sizable population of settlers. In other parts of Africa, the French and English were largely bureaucrats. As a result, a third of the cocoa, coffee, and banana plantations were in the hands of French citizens. A forced labor system, much hated by the Africans, became the backbone of the economy. At the time of independence, Côte d'Ivoire was French West Africa's most prosperous country, accounting for over 40% of the region's total exports.

WISH FOR INDEPENDENCE

After World War I, the French paid greater attention to the provision of education, health services, development assistance, and the safeguarding of local land rights. But it was too late. During the war years, a nationalist movement began to emerge, and the wish for independence grew. In 1944 a Baule chief, Félix Houphouët-Boigny, founded a union of Ivorian farmers, the African Agricultural Union. This organization had several objectives—to secure better prices for African products, eliminate practices that benefited European farmers, and abolish forced labor.

From this organization emerged the first major African political party, the Democratic Party of Côte d'Ivoire (PDCI), led by Houphouët-Boigny. The PDCI met with opposition from the French administration because such a nationalistic party threatened French control. Tensions escalated into violence in 1949. Houphouët-Boigny then reversed his nationalistic policy and began to cooperate with the French. On December 4, 1958, Côte d'Ivoire was proclaimed a republic by the French. After national elections in 1959, Houphouët-Boigny became premier. In 1960 he was elected president.

INDEPENDENCE AND ITS AFTERMATH

After Houphouët-Boigny became the country's first president, his government gave farmers good prices for their cash crops to stimulate production further. The focus of development was on methods to improve farming. Coffee production increased significantly—Côte d'Ivoire is now the world's third largest producer annually of coffee, after Brazil and Colombia. Cocoa production achieved similar results. By 1979 the country was the world's leading cocoa producer. It also became Africa's leading exporter of pineapples and palm oil. This "Ivorian miracle" was created with the help of French bureaucrats. In the rest of Africa, Europeans were driven out by the people following independence, but in Côte d'Ivoire, they poured in, the result of Houphouët-Boigny's efforts to secure grants of French aid and attract a large number of French business interests. The French community grew from 10,000 to 50,000. Most of them were teachers and advisors.

After independence, Côte d'Ivoire was ruled by a one-party regime. Houphouët-Boigny's Democratic Party was the only legal party, and all members of the executive and legislative branches pledged allegiance to it. A free press did not exist—the only newspapers were government-owned. Opposition parties were outlawed, and freedom of expression, whether oral or written, was prohibited.

As long as the economy prospered, Ivorians did not complain loudly about the lack of liberties. For 20 years, throughout the 1960s and 1970s, the economy maintained an annual growth rate of 10%, and the infrequent protests against the president's conservatism never merited military intervention. In 1973, a conspiracy by army officers was thwarted; in 1980, an attempt on the president's life was made; and in 1983, student unrest caused the closure of the university in Abidjan.

Opposite: **A farmer harvests his oil palms. Formerly a taxi driver, this man was drawn back into farming because of the higher profits.**

PROTESTS AND DEMOCRACY

In 1986 the economic situation worsened. Coffee and cocoa prices dropped, and a world recession followed. People voiced their displeasure with the government, demanded greater respect for human rights, and renewed their interest in a multiparty parliamentary democracy.

The external debt and crime in Abidjan both increased threefold. The government took measures to restore economic growth, but these actions were not welcomed by the general public because they did not improve the standard of living for most people. At the peak of the economic crisis, President Houphouët-Boigny was forced to call in the International Monetary Fund (IMF) for help on debt payment. Hundreds of civil servants went on strike, and students joined in violent street protests, resulting in five student deaths. The unrest was unparalleled in its scale and vigor. An investigating committee concluded that the military was responsible for the deaths, but the government refused to take action. As a result, people began to riot. After months of instability, Houphouët-Boigny was forced to legitimize other political parties and allow independent newspapers to begin publishing.

Houphouët-Boigny was elected to his seventh term in 1990, even though the elections were opened to other political parties for the first time. However, he received only 85% of the vote instead of the usual 99.9%. He died in office in 1993 and was peacefully replaced by his hand-picked successor, the speaker of the National Assembly, Henri Konan-Bédié. Konan-Bédié won the election in 1995.

Diners at a presidential banquet. By 1990 the political situation took a turn for the worse and the economic crisis was blamed on corruption and the extravagant lifestyle of officials.

HOUPHOUËT-BOIGNY

Félix Houphouët-Boigny studied medicine before becoming a prosperous cocoa farmer and local chief. In 1944 he turned to politics and formed the country's first agricultural trade union, whose members consisted of African planters. Annoyed that colonial policy favored French plantation owners, they united to recruit migrant workers for their own farms. A year later, the French abolished forced labor. Houphouët-Boigny attracted notice and within a year was elected to the French Parliament in Paris. He gradually dropped the more radical stance of his youth when he was associated with international Marxist organizations. France rewarded this change by eventually appointing him as the first African to become a minister in a European government.

When Côte d'Ivoire achieved independence, Houphouët-Boigny installed himself in virtual permanent power. He skillfully managed a personality cult by periodically granting amnesty to those in prison for less violent crimes and to political prisoners who had tried to oust him from office. He was a popular figure in Ivorian politics despite his sponsorship of huge building projects in the 1980s, such as the building of the basilica, Our Lady of Peace, while the country's economy was in a slump. Houphouët-Boigny is remembered for the economic and political growth he brought to the country. At his death in 1993, he was genuinely mourned by Ivorians.

Left: **An Ivorian woman proudly wears a dress with a picture of Félix Houphouët-Boigny.**

GOVERNMENT

FROM INDEPENDENCE TO 1990, Côte d'Ivoire had a one-party government. All candidates for the national assembly belonged to the Democratic Party of Côte d'Ivoire (PDCI), which was considered the only legal party. In 1990, however, other parties were legalized. Today Côte d'Ivoire is a multiparty republic with an independent judiciary and national legislature.

LOCAL GOVERNMENT

Côte d'Ivoire is divided into 10 regions, each ruled by a regional governor. These regions are further divided into 40 subregions, led by deputy governors. Governors are nominated by the Ministry of the Interior and appointed by the president.

Opposite: **Former president Houphouët-Boigny at the entrance to his palace. In his hand is a gold-plated sword. The sword is his family symbol and the translation of his Baule name.**

POLITICAL STRUCTURE

EXECUTIVE POWER is exercised by the elected president and chief of state—Henri Konan-Bédié since 1993. The president appoints a prime minister as head of his government. The prime minister, in turn, appoints a ministerial cabinet to carry out the work of the government and introduce legislation to the National Assembly.

JUDICIAL POWER is based on French civil law, with the highest level of authority in the hands of the Supreme Court. A high court of justice has the authority to try government officials, even the president. Lower courts include the appellate or court of appeals, state security, and court of first instance.

LEGISLATIVE POWER is exerted by the National Assembly, which is run like a parliament. Its 175 members are elected by direct popular vote to serve five-year terms. In 1995, 14 seats were won by women.

ELECTORAL SYSTEM

Number of constituencies

175 constituencies

Voting system

– Simple majority vote in one round
– Vacancies arising between general elections are filled by by-elections held within three months. No by-election is held within the last 12 months of the legislature
– Voting is not compulsory

Voter requirements

– Age: 21 years
– Côte d'Ivoire citizenship
– Full possession of civil and political rights
– Disqualifications: insanity, conviction for crime

Candidate eligibility

– Age: 23 years
– Côte d'Ivoire citizenship
– Ineligibility: guardianship, work undertaken for and financed by a foreign state or international organization, executive in a national enterprise, or one benefiting from state concessions

DEMOCRATIC DEMANDS

Prior to 1995, the PDCI maintained its political dominance despite multiparty presidential and legislative elections in 1990. In October 1995, major opposition parties boycotted the presidential election, citing irregularities in the electoral code and voter registration. They claimed that the government used the 1994 electoral code to place formidable obstacles in the path of political rivals. One of the opposition parties, the Rally of Republicans (RDR), held that Alassane Ouattara, a leading rival to Bédié, had been unfairly excluded from entering the presidential race. The opposition also complained that there were not enough checks to ensure that voters were eligible, and that there were unfair restrictions on demonstrations after the government issued a three-month ban on marches and sit-ins prior to the election in an attempt to guarantee public order. The opposition called for an active boycott of the presidential election. They blocked access to polling stations and prevented delivery of election materials. Talks between the government and opposition groups broke down over this issue, despite concessions on both sides. At least five people were killed.

In early November, negotiations between the government and the opposition parties led to an agreement in which the controversial electoral lists would be revised. As a result, the boycott was lifted, and nine opposition parties challenged the ruling PDCI for the 175 parliamentary seats. A number of independent candidates, some of whom had left the PDCI, also joined the race.

One of the many government buildings in Abidjan.

ASSEMBLY ELECTION RESULTS

> *"When a regime is bad, we have to combat it with whatever means possible in order to achieve change and remove dictators."*
>
> — *Laurent Gbagbo, leader of the Ivorian Popular Front*

For the 1995 election, the main opposition parties were grouped under the Republican Front (FR). There were active boycotts, and ethnic violence occurred between the Bete and the Baule. As a result, the voting in three of the 175 constituencies had to be rescheduled. Despite the chaos, however, foreign observers acting as monitors considered the actual voting a smooth process. This contrasted with the tension that had surrounded the presidential election. The final results saw the PDCI winning an overwhelming majority of 80% of the seats in the national assembly. A new cabinet was named on January 26, 1996.

Many observers attribute the opposition's poor results to the disunity among the opposition parties and their inability to present coalition candidates. The ruling party undoubtedly gained the people's vote by President Bédié's ability to produce favorable economic results. By 1995, the economy was improving significantly.

AMNESTY INTERNATIONAL REPORT

Amnesty International reported before the 1995 election that "violations of the right to freedom of expression and association" were occurring in Côte d'Ivoire. They pointed to arrests and convictions of students and journalists as evidence of their concern. A particular target was the Federation of Students and School Pupils (FESCI), many of whose members were arrested after clashes with the police. One such member at the executive level, Eugene Gonthy, considered a prisoner of conscience by Amnesty International, was sent to prison in 1996 for two years. One of the lawyers defending active boycott members alleged that approximately 100 of an estimated 450 such persons arrested were still detained two years after their arrest, awaiting judicial action. Of those tried and sentenced, six died in prison, 12 accepted a presidential pardon, six were released on provisional liberty and had their sentences overturned, nine are serving their sentences, and 95 have completed their sentences. Figures on active boycott members published in the government-controlled newspaper are significantly lower.

POLITICAL UNREST

Constitutional reforms introduced by President Bédié and adopted by parliament in June 1998 drew much criticism from the Republican Front and professional groups such as teachers. Bédié extended the presidential mandate from five to seven years and bestowed on himself the power to withhold election results when there is unrest in the country. He also has the power to nominate one-third of the members of a newly-created senate.

The Republican Front expected at least one million supporters to join them in a protest against these undemocratic laws. They knew this demonstration would be seen as provocative by the government, but nevertheless, it was a test of the ruling party's contention that they were democratic. In anticipation of trouble, 1,000 police officers were mobilized to control the protesters, if needed. However, this was unnecessary as Bédié, instead of listening to the concerns of the demonstrators, left the country to visit South Africa on the day of the march. Protesters felt his departure proved that he wanted to avoid stirring up trouble in the country.

Soldiers returning from army maneuvers. Three million Ivorian men, between the ages of 15 and 49, are eligible for compulsory military service.

MILITARY AND SECURITY FORCES

The nation's army has seven battalions—four infantry, one armored, one antiaircraft artillery, and one engineering. Because of increased, violent incursions by Liberians in 1998, the government designated Liberian border districts as part of a military operational zone, where the armed forces are responsible for all security matters.

Besides the army, the country has a navy with warships, auxiliaries, and service craft. The air force has one fighter bomber squadron and 20 transport aircraft. There is also a presidential guard and militia.

Security forces include the national police, the *surete* ("SUR-eh-tay"), and a paramilitary national *gendarmerie* ("SHON-dar-mer-ee"), a branch of the armed forces responsible for general law enforcement in rural areas. A new National Security Council was formed in 1998 to coordinate security policy, both internal and external. In the same year, the Special Anti-Crime Police Brigade (SAVAC), which focuses on internal security, and specifically violent crime, began its operations.

FREEDOM OF SPEECH AND ASSEMBLY

Although the constitution provides for freedom of expression, the government does not tolerate what it considers insults or attacks on the honor of the country's highest officials, and such offenses are punishable by prison sentences. Some teachers who are active in opposition politics report that they have been transferred because of their political activities.

The constitution also provides for freedom of assembly. In practice, however, that freedom is restricted whenever the government perceives a danger to public order. Groups that wish to hold demonstrations or rallies are required to submit a notice to the Ministry of Security or Interior 48 hours before the proposed event. The government sometimes denies the opposition permission to meet in public, outdoor locations. Following opposition demonstrations in September 1995, the government announced that "all marches and sit-ins would be banned for a three-month period in all streets and public places." The decree was selectively applied—only opposition events were affected. Penalties for infraction ranged from no action to 12 months' imprisonment. An "antivandalism" law, passed by the national assembly in 1992, holds organizers of a march or demonstration responsible if any of the participants engage in violence.

In 1991 the government banned the previously registered student union FESCI after a student was killed by other students, but FESCI remains active in demonstrations, ceremonies, and political party conventions. In December 1996 the police broke up an informal memorial service organized by students and held on the university campus. On December 19, four FESCI leaders appeared at the office of the Minister of Security, reportedly at his invitation, but were arrested. On January 7, 1997, three of the four were convicted and sentenced to two years in prison under the "antivandalism" law and laws against disturbing the public order.

The National Security Council is headed by the former chief of the gendarmerie.

HUMAN RIGHTS ORGANIZATIONS

The Ivorian League for the Rights of Man, formed in March 1987, is the main organization in the country that promotes and protects Ivorians' human rights, including those in prisons. Membership is diverse, composed of activists and people from various professions. There are 750 members, and the group has no office of its own. Its headquarters is in Abidjan, and members meet and work in a church. The organization has sought to open branches in Abidjan and other parts of the country. It now has four branches in Abidjan and 14 in the whole nation. Since its creation, the Ivorian League has denounced human rights violations in the country by press releases, conferences, and appeals to external partners (in Africa and farther). When it receives a complaint, it contacts the person whose rights have been violated, makes investigations, tracks down witnesses, and negotiates with the violator to bring an end to the violation. If no agreement is reached, it will take the case to court.

In 1992, after gross violations of human rights at the University of Abidjan, the League, along with some political parties, organized a public protest in the streets of Abidjan. The police violently suppressed this demonstration, and arrested the secretary-general of the organization and imprisoned him for several months.

The Christian Association for the Abolition of Torture and Respect for Human Rights was established in 1990. The organization, composed of students, lawyers, schoolchildren, teachers, and others, has approximately 300 members. Their stated main objective is the promotion and protection of human rights and to continue the struggle against torture. They sponsor campaigns, hold seminars and workshops, and plan to open a documentation center on human rights. The association has observer status with the African Commission on Human and Peoples' Rights. Its headquarters is in Abidjan, and the organization has no office space of its own.

Research and Study Group on Democracy and Development in Africa (Côte d'Ivoire Branch) is a pan-African, nonprofit organization created in 1990. Its headquarters is in Benin, and there are over 1,000 members in 20 African countries. The group's main objective is the monitoring of democracy through civic education, training of election observers, research, and political intermediation. Membership consists of intellectuals from all professions. There is an office in Abidjan.

HUMAN RIGHTS ABUSE

The government has cooperated with international inquiries into its human rights practices, but various human rights organizations have alleged that, although there has been some improvement, serious abuses continue. The judiciary, although theoretically independent, is subject to executive branch influence and does not always ensure due process.

With a high rate of violent civil crimes, the security forces are said to have a shoot-to-kill policy when pursuing criminal suspects. Corpses of alleged criminals killed by SAVAC or police personnel are regularly displayed on television and in the newspapers. The government has not prosecuted SAVAC or police personnel for any of these killings.

The Ivorian Navy guarding the shores.

WIDER AFFILIATIONS

The Ivorian government has, in the past, acted as mediator in conflicts in other parts of Africa. In 1997 President Bédié met with the Angolan leader, Jonas Savimbi, to encourage him to cooperate with the United Nations in the implementation of the Angola peace process. President Bédié also visited South Africa in 1998 at the invitation of President Nelson Mandela. The aim was to consolidate existing trade and economic relations between the two countries, which are two of the larger economies in Africa. Bédié's visit was depicted by the Ivorian official press as a sign of the changing political climate in Africa as a whole.

Côte d'Ivoire is a member of the Economic Community of West African States (ECOWAS) and supports the organization's efforts to have a regional military force as a future peacekeeping body. ECOWAS and the Organization of African Unity (OAU), a political organization that aims to promote unity among African countries, improve living standards, and establish international cooperation, are robustly supported by the majority of Ivorians. They are viewed as successful efforts to provide a framework for African nations to cooperate with each other in promoting peace and democracy.

PRESIDENT HENRI KONAN-BÉDIÉ

Bédié was born in Dadiekro in central Côte d'Ivoire in 1934. He attended schools in Côte d'Ivoire and France before completing a doctoral degree in economics from the University of Poitiers in France.

In 1960, during the last remaining months of his country's colonialization, he entered the civil service and served as a diplomatic counselor at the French embassy in the United States. For the next six years, he was the first Ivorian ambassador to the United States. In January 1966 he returned home to accept appointment as a minister delegate for financial affairs. He was soon promoted to Minister of Economy and Finance. At the same time he acted as governor of the International Monetary Fund and administrator for the World Bank.

In June 1977, after being dismissed from his ministry following the bankruptcy of six state-owned sugar factories, Bédié became special advisor for African affairs to the president of the International Finance Cooperation of the World Bank in Washington, D.C. When he returned home in December 1980, Bédié was elected president of the new national assembly. He became acting president of the country in 1993 after the death of Houphouët-Boigny.

In October 1995 Bédié won the election after achieving some notable successes during his term, for instance, the reduction of crime. However, he has been criticized for human rights abuse and hostility toward the independent press, which has found fault with his policies.

Like his mentor, President Houphouët-Boigny, President Henri Konan-Bédié is also a Baule.

Opposite: **President Seng-hor of Senegal (right) greets President Houp-houët-Boigny at Dakar airport in 1977. Since the 1970s, the nation has been working towards cementing relations with its neighbors.**

ECONOMY

THE ECONOMY OF CÔTE D'IVOIRE relies primarily on agriculture. There have been some very hard times during the past 15 years because of the economy's dependence on the volatile international commodity market. As a result, the country has had difficulty in paying its foreign debt. Côte d'Ivoire has made some difficult economic decisions, and is now in a better position to take advantage of the global marketplace.

Numerous government enterprises have become part of the private sector, but there remains a lot of government participation through investment and tax policies. Multinational corporations are forming partnerships with Ivorian-owned companies. There is a growing enthusiasm among American businessmen to invest in Côte d'Ivoire, as the country opens its doors to all investors. Future growth of the economy will depend on the availability of investment funds and energy sources, and the size of world markets.

Opposite: **An Ivorian woman harvesting rice. Although rice is one of the country's agricultural products, many Ivorians prefer to eat imported rice.**

Left: **A farmer takes his cattle to the market.**

Côte d'Ivoire is the second most indebted country in the world with a debt of US$19 billion. In first place is Nigeria, with debts amounting to US$35 billion.

DEVASTATING DEBT

Most African countries do not have the money to develop their economies. Foreign private enterprise has often considered investment in these underdeveloped areas too risky. Thus the major alternative sources of financing are national and multinational lending institutions.

In 1995 an agreement was reached between Côte d'Ivoire, and the International Monetary Fund (IMF) and the World Bank to forego 50% of its foreign debt and reschedule the rest as part of a structural adjustment package. In return for the implemention of strict reforms by the Ivorian government, the IMF and World Bank agreed to supply a debt-relief package totaling US$800 million.

The reforms require the end of state-mandated cocoa prices to farmers. A government marketing board, which used to be responsible for setting cocoa prices for middlemen who sell to government-approved export companies, was abolished. Starting in 1999 the government board will only be used for information and research. The market will also be opened up. Because of uncertainty over the new system, many companies turned to processing cocoa. The entry of multinationals into this sector has led to an increase in processing capacity. This development means more jobs, more advanced technology, and an improvement in the industrial base.

THE INTERNATIONAL MONETARY FUND (IMF) AND THE WORLD BANK

Both the IMF and World Bank are governed by ministers of committees representing the 22 major economies of the world. The IMF lends money when member countries, typically developing countries, encounter balance of payment problems, and accepting a loan means big, internal economic changes. The World Bank loans money to developing countries for particular projects. World Bank and IMF programs are intended to benefit the world's poorest countries with the aim to free resources for spending in the crucial areas of health, education, and rural development.

DIVERSIFYING THE ECONOMY

To end the country's dependence on fluctuating world prices for cocoa and coffee, Côte d'Ivoire aims to process half of all the raw materials it produces before exporting them. As a result, a light industrial sector has emerged, producing textiles, chemicals, and sugar for export. A few assembly plants for cars and other manufactured goods have also been built and have made significant headway. Currently, approximately 20% of all agricultural products, such as coffee and cocoa, are processed before export. The export rate is even higher for rubber and palm oil, an essential ingredient in the preparation of African food.

Despite government moves to expand the economy, agriculture, forestry, and related activities retain their prime importance. Together they employ approximately 85% of the working population. They are the major export earners (80 to 95% of total exports) and the second largest contributor to the country's Gross Domestic Product (GDP), after the service sector.

The fruit of the oil palm being crushed to produce palm oil. Côte d'Ivoire was once the world's third largest exporter of palm oil. However, with the aging of the plantations, the export volume has decreased significantly.

Above: **Villagers grading coffee beans before packing them. Coffee is the favorite business for almost all families in the southeast.**

Opposite: **Canned tuna on display in a shop. The country is a major exporter of tuna.**

AGRICULTURE

Côte d'Ivoire is the world's largest producer of cocoa and has a 42% share of the world market. More than a quarter of the population is engaged in the production of cocoa. The country is also the leading African producer of coffee. These two commodities make up half of the country's export earnings. Besides cocoa and coffee, the government encourages the production of cotton, bananas, rubber, rice, and sugar. Along the coast, pineapple and coconut trees are also grown.

A variety of vegetables are grown, including rice, yams, cassava, okra, sweet potatoes, peppers, and plantain bananas. Cassava, more commonly known as tapioca, is widely grown because it does well on eroded soils.

Despite such massive production, Côte d'Ivoire is among the top 10 importers of food in Africa. This is because cultivated land is primarily used for commercial cash crops, and people farm on a subsistence basis. Goats and sheep are the most significant livestock raised, since cows cannot be bred in areas infested with tsetse flies.

MANUFACTURING

The larger manufacturing industries include food-processing plants, lumber and textile mills, car assembly plants, oil refineries, and steel container and aluminum sheet production. An important sector of the economy is oil refining. Côte d'Ivoire, unlike some African countries, does not have huge supplies of oil. Offshore oil was discovered in large quantities in 1977, and production began in 1980. The annual output is currently about 2.5 million barrels.

The country's chemical industry centers around rubber, as there are a number of rubber plantations that mainly export latex. The government used to have a large stake in the three major companies involved in this industry, but has sold its shares to private interests in the move to privatization.

FORESTRY

Côte d'Ivoire is a major exporter of hardwood. In the mid-1970s, timber overtook coffee to become the principal export. Since then, more sawmills and wood-processing plants have been built to produce plywood, crates, boxes, veneer, cabinets, and furniture. These finished products are exported to Europe and the United States.

The President Hotel in Yamoussoukro is a typical example of the luxurious hotels that have been built, thanks to the booming tourist industry.

MINING

Although there are known reserves of copper, nickel, uranium, and manganese, mining is not a booming industry in Côte d'Ivoire. About 12,000 carats of diamonds are produced each year. The diamonds are exploited on the Bou tributary of the Bandama river. Gold mining began in early 1990. Besides diamonds and gold, petroleum is also pumped from three offshore fields.

TOURISM

With a long strip of beautiful beaches, lagoons, protected wildlife, and a rich cultural heritage, Côte d'Ivoire has plenty to offer tourists. Tourism has the potential to be a leading industry, but a lot more resources have to be put into the building of hotels and tourist attractions. The present government regards the further development of the tourist industry as its key priority.

A timber mill in San-Pédro. Côte d'Ivoire is a major exporter of tropical wood and processed timber products.

TRADE

Foreign trade consists of imports of petroleum products, consumer goods, machinery, and transportation equipment and exports of coffee, cocoa, and timber. In 1995 annual exports totaled $3.7 billion, and imports amounted to $2.4 billion. Principal trading partners for exports are the Netherlands, France, Germany, and the United States. Chief partners for imports are France, Nigeria, Germany, Italy, and the United States. Principal imports from the United States are paper products, computer hardware and software, cosmetics, and toiletries.

CURRENCY

Côte d'Ivoire is a member of the six-nation West African Monetary Union. The currency is the African Financial Community (CFA) franc with convertibility guaranteed by the French treasury. In 1993, before devaluation, 285 CFA francs equaled US$1, but by 1998, it was 607 to a dollar.

INFRASTRUCTURE

Côte d'Ivoire has a very good infrastructure by the standards of developing countries. Eight percent of the 43,000 miles (68,000 km) of highways are paved, and there are good telecommunications, two modern ports, rail and air links, and modern housing developments. The port of Abidjan is one of the busiest in West Africa, and a new port operates in San-Pédro. A railroad links the interior with main cities and other countries. The total length of operated railroad track is about 410 miles (660 km).

The construction and maintenance of roads has been privatized to improve efficiency and the condition of roads. Some dirt roads, which become impassable during the rainy season, have been replaced with paved roads. Abidjan has an international airport located at Port-Bouët. About a dozen foreign airline companies, including Air Afrique, a service maintained by some French-speaking African countries, use its facilities regularly. The national airline, Air Ivoire, serves airports and landing fields that are scattered across the country.

MEETING GROWING ENERGY NEEDS

As more people migrate to the cities, energy needs increase dramatically. Côte d'Ivoire used to import electricity from Ghana, but after the discovery of a plentiful supply of offshore natural gas and the construction of modern power stations, Côte d'Ivoire now produces enough electricity for its own needs and is an exporter of electricity as well.

Before the discovery of natural gas, the annual production of electricity in the early 1990s totaled about two billion kilowatt-hours—much of it generated by hydroelectric installations. Hydroelectric plants are located on the Bia and Bandama rivers. Although Africa has about 40% of the world's hydropower potential, only a relatively small portion has been developed due to high construction costs, inaccessibility of sites, and their distance from markets.

The Ivorian energy minister has proposed the building of a gas pipeline from Côte d'Ivoire to a new power plant in Ghana. This marks the beginning of a regional West African gas link-up with Côte d'Ivoire and Nigeria as the biggest suppliers. The plan, an exciting development for the region, would supply five countries with natural gas within a regional energy pool.

USE OF SOLAR POWER

Using renewable energy to improve the quality and to speed up the drying of cocoa is catching on in Côte d'Ivoire. For cooperatives participating in the pilot project, solar-powered bean dryers will be installed in greenhouses with the aim of reducing moisture in the cocoa to exportable levels and therefore increasing the amount of grade-one cocoa. There is concern in the industry that because of the many private regulators now licensed to check quality, there is poorer quality cocoa. When buyers are eager to meet exporters' demands during the peak harvesting period of October to February, farmers sometimes sell damp crop, which turns moldy easily. Beans for export arriving at Abidjan at the start of the 1997–98 season had much higher humidity levels than in previous years.

WORKING CONDITIONS

The legal minimum working age in Côte d'Ivoire is 16, and the Ministry of Employment and Civil Service strictly enforces this provision in the civil service and in multinational companies. There are reports, however, of adolescents under 16 working in small workshops. A monthly minimum wage, last adjusted after the devaluation of the CFA franc in January 1994, is imposed by the government. This rate is enforced for salaried workers employed by the government or registered with the social security office. A slightly higher minimum wage applies to construction workers. The minimum wage varies according to occupation, with the lowest set at US$71.49 (43,394 CFA francs) per month. This meager amount is hardly enough to provide a decent standard of living for a family. The majority of the labor force works in agriculture, forestry, or in the

Unlike urban workers *(opposite)*, farmers *(right)*, who grow crops to sell in markets, usually do not have a steady income.

informal sector where minimum wage rules do not apply.

Through the Ministry of Employment and the Civil Service, the government enforces a comprehensive labor code governing the terms and conditions of service for wage earners and salaried workers. Those employed in the formal sector are reasonably protected against unjust compensation, excessive hours, and arbitrary discharge from employment. The standard legal work week is 40 hours. The law requires overtime payment on a graduated scale for additional hours. The code provides for at least one, 24-hour rest period per week. Government labor inspectors can order employers to improve substandard conditions, and a labor court can levy fines if the employer fails to comply. The code also provides for occupational safety and health standards. In the large informal sector of the economy, however, the government's occupational health and safety regulations are enforced erratically at best.

The labor code grants all citizens, except members of the police and military, the right to join unions, call strikes, and to bargain collectively. About 100,000 workers belong to 190 unions grouped together in the government-sponsored General Workers Union.

IVORIANS

IN THE RURAL PARTS OF THE COUNTRY, the Ivorian culture, in terms of food, religion, dress, tribal roles, and daily life, has remained unchanged for hundreds of years. There has been a shift of social identity, however. Ivorians now consider themselves citizens of Côte d'Ivoire first, then as members of their ethnic groups.

POPULATION CHARACTERISTICS

Côte d'Ivoire has about 15 million people, with an annual growth rate of 2.35%, one of the highest in the world. Half the population is less than 16 years old. Besides the indigenous people, who make up 70% of the population, there are non-Africans, mostly French and Lebanese. These people form 3% of the population. The remaining 27% are Africans who are either immigrant workers or refugees who fled to Côte d'Ivoire as a result of civil war in neighboring countries.

Opposite: **Children from the town of Daloa in ritual dress pose for a picture before performing a dance.**

Left: **Ivorians washing laundry in a river. This organized laundry business is a common sight near Abidjan.**

INDIGENOUS PEOPLE

Culturally, Côte d'Ivoire is a diverse ethnic puzzle with over 60 ethnic groups. The major groups came relatively recently from neighboring countries—the Malinke people came after the collapse of the Mali empire in the 16th century; the Kru people migrated from Liberia around 1600; and the Senufo and Lobi tribes moved southward from Burkina Faso and Mali. It was not until the 18th and 19th centuries that the Akan people, the Baule, Agni, and Abron, migrated from Ghana into the eastern and central areas of the country. Around the same time, the Dioula moved from Guinea into the northwest.

THE BAULE are the largest ethnic group in Côte d'Ivoire. They live in the central part of the country, producing primarily coffee and cocoa. The Baule have a matrilineal social structure, although men occupy the important leadership positions, and are expected to support children of a deceased maternal relative, such as a sister. Baule villages are united into chiefdoms with the chief acting as protector, priest, judge, and ruler. It is a humanistic society—people, not material wealth, come first. A Baule would not say to a sibling, "Go to *my* room and get *my* jacket," but instead, "Go to *the* room and get *the* jacket." The possessive pronoun "my," does not exist.

THE AGNI AND ABRON migrated from the east and established powerful kingdoms on the fringes of the forest. Agni and Abron kings still receive allegiance from their people, adapting to modern institutions when necessary. Every Friday at the king's palace, the sacred throne is shown to the people. Also on this day, the king teaches history to young people and counsels his people. Family descent is through the maternal line like

Former Ivorian president Félix Houphouët-Boigny disliked the matrilineal aspect of Baule society. He thought it was a cause of family disunity.

the Baule, and polygamy for the male is the custom. Because they have retained their traditional monarchy, these people enjoy an elite status and political power in Côte d'Ivoire. The tribes' main livelihood is subsistence farming with an emphasis on growing important cash crops such as cocoa and coffee. They mostly live in small villages and towns and are famous for their artwork with metal, wood, and clay.

THE DAN OR YACOUBA tribe is one of the most interesting tribes in the country. The word "Yacouba" in the local dialect means, "all that begins by animated discussion." The Dan are noted for their dance masks, and dances are held to mark all the important life events. So, it is not surprising that some of the best dancers in the country come from this tribe. Besides masks, the Dan are also well known for other crafts, including woven cloth, basketry, and wooden sculpture.

A tribal chief with his subjects during a royal wedding.

51

THE SENUFO live in small villages of circular huts in the northern savanna. Considered the oldest ethnic group in Cote d'Ivoire, they settled in this place around 1600. Although famous for their woodcarving, masks, hand-painted Korhogo fabrics, pottery, dance, and music, the Senufo are predominantly an agricultural people, cultivating rice, yams, peanuts, and millet. The close relationship between the Senufo farmer and his land can be seen in their religious observances. Each village has a mythical ancestor in the form of an animal. This animal or totem is special to the Senufo and is a symbol of unity. The head of the family is the main authority figure who intercedes with the gods on behalf of his family to ensure good harvests. Aside from the lineage head, status distinctions are relatively few, although many people kept slaves from other societies until well into the 20th century. The Senufo consider everyone in the village to be part of an extended family. Everyone in a village will eat and farm together. Food is stored collectively, and each family contributes to the village.

Korhogo, the capital of the Senufo people, is over 311 miles (500 km) north of Abidjan and dates from the 13th century. The Senufo have secret associations—the Poro cult for boys and the Sakrobundi cult for girls. These groups help prepare the children for adulthood. The goal is to preserve the group's folklore, teach tribal customs, and instill self-control through rigorous tests. The children's education is divided into three seven-year periods, ending with an initiation ceremony involving circumcision, isolation, and the instruction and use of masks. Each community has a sacred forest where the training is done, and the uninitiated are not allowed to visit. However, they may watch the dance of the leopard men, a dance performed when the boys return from a training session in the forest. Ceremonies and dances mark the passage from one stage to the next. When a man is 30 years old, he is finally considered an adult and an elder who can offer advice to his people.

The existence of the Poro was at one time threatened by schools, which teach a different system of thought and occupy a large portion of a child's life. The problem, however, was solved by combining the teachings of the school with the laws, beliefs, and secrets of the Poro.

Opposite: **An artisan weaving cloth at a weaving center. Korhogo is famous for its fabrics.**

THE DIOULA live in the far northwest. They came from Guinea, bringing with them the Islamic faith. In addition to trading, their major activity, the Dioula are subsistence farmers of rice, millet, and peanuts. They also keep goats, sheep, poultry, and some cattle. This is a patrilineal society with the oldest male as head of his lineage. Villages tend to be grouped around men with the same clan name, and headmen are called imams or religious leaders. Men hunt and do the heavy farm work, while women tend to the children, as well as domestic and farm chores. Marriages are arranged with a price paid to the bride's family, and some men have up to three wives.

There are three classes within the Dioula—the free born, originally considered the nobility but today consisting of farmers, merchants, and Muslim clerics; the artisan class of blacksmiths and leather workers; and the *griots* ("GREE-ohs"), responsible for passing down oral tradition and cultural heritage to succeeding generations. Oral literature is strong because few are literate.

A blend of Islam and traditional beliefs has resulted in healing and magic becoming very important. Holy men are called on for protective charms or to put a curse on an enemy. Although many Dioula conceal their belief in magic, almost all carry a charm.

The Lobi and the Kulango remain extremely steadfast in their religions and traditions. When Islam was introduced to the country, they resisted it. They have rejected many aspects of European acculturation and lack the overall fascination with economic progress that characterizes much of the nation.

THE LOBI live close to the Senufo in an isolated, relatively undeveloped part of the country. A proud people, they are known for their superb archery skills. The young boys are taught archery, their training divided into seven-year periods, so that by age 21, they are able to hunt big game. Lobi women adorn themselves with ornamental plates that pierce through their lips.

Unlike many of the ethnic groups, the Lobi have clung tightly to their traditions and seem uninterested in what is happening in the rest of the country.

THE KULANGO are closely related to the Lobi, their former enemies. They occupy the same region and share similar languages, customs, lifestyles, and religious beliefs. The Kulango are primarily farmers, growing crops such as yams, corn, peanuts, cotton, and watermelons. Some of them also breed goats, sheep, and cattle. The women gather wild fruits and nuts, while the men do most of the agricultural work.

Each Kulango village is made up of several small settlements of mud huts. The huts are grouped around a center court, which serves as a meeting place. Every settlement consists of several extended families, and each family has an economic unit. The male head of each extended family is responsible for offering sacrifices to the ancestral spirits. He is succeeded by his oldest sister's eldest son. The village head and the religious chief handle all disputes and community affairs.

Most Kulango girls are betrothed while they are quite young. Marriages are arranged by either the girl's father or the extended family head. When a man marries, his bride may either join him or remain in her father's home. If she remains with her father, her daughters live with her, and her sons join their father when they are able to walk and talk.

THE KRU have a long association with the sea. Fishing is their major activity. Traditionally the men loaded logging ships and made long sea passages with their cargoes. The Kru have tried to maintain their autonomy, but this has proved difficult and they are becoming more assimilated into the mainstream. Nevertheless, their traditional oral culture, accounting for numerous folk stories and morality tales, remains strong. Kru families are patrilineal, and marriage is polygamous. Not known to have kept slaves themselves, they exported slaves from neighboring tribes during the height of the slave trade.

MINORITIES

Non-Ivorian Africans who reside in Côte d'Ivoire make up almost one-third of the total population. Their numbers are growing as quickly as the crime rate, thus many Ivorians attribute the high crime rate to these foreigners. As a result, foreign Africans are often subject to discrimination, sometimes even harassment.

Workers unload tuna from a fishing boat in Abidjan. Today fishing is no longer a profitable business for the Kru as their local port, Tabou, has declined in importance, compared to the ports of Abidjan and San-Pédro.

REFUGEES

There are currently 305,000 Liberian refugees living in Côte d'Ivoire. The Liberian civil war killed 10% of its 2.5 million people and made refugees of another 700,000. People were driven out of their communities and into five neighboring West African countries. The Ivorian government cooperates with the UN High Commissioner for Refugees in health, education, and food distribution programs for refugees. It also agreed in principle to permit Liberians to cast absentee ballots should elections take place in their homeland.

In April 1998 serious factional fighting in Monrovia, a Liberian city, caused thousands of its residents to seek escape. On May 7, the *Bulk Challenger*, a Nigerian freighter carrying up to 3,500 passengers, arrived at San-Pédro. UN and voluntary agencies expressed concern that the conditions on board could pose a threat to the lives of the passengers. The government allowed most of the women and children to disembark temporarily. However, it did not authorize any screening of the passengers for refugee status. Government officials cited a threat to national security, alleging that factional fighters were on board. In reality, they feared that more ships bearing asylum seekers would follow. After making repairs to the ship, the *Bulk Challenger* was ordered to reboard its passengers and sail for Ghana. There were several reports of deaths before the ship reached Ghana, where its passengers were granted asylum.

IVORIAN CHARACTER

Respect for one's family, elderly people, and women, is a distinctive quality of Ivorian people. Ivorians are very hospitable people—they are always ready to welcome strangers into their homes for some food and drink. They are also extremely polite and like to inquire about one's health and family. Ivorians are gentle people and are often laid-back. To the Ivorian, trust is very important in a relationship, whether one of business or friendship. Without trust, nothing can be done.

SOCIAL CUSTOMS

In the traditional Ivorian greeting it is important to inquire about a person's health, family, work, or the weather. Getting down to business immediately is considered rude. Women do not shake hands with each other but instead kiss each other three times on the cheeks, starting with the left cheek and alternating sides. Men, however, typically shake hands. At social functions, it is polite to shake hands with everyone when entering and again when leaving. Eye contact is usually avoided, particularly between father and child. It is considered extremely rude to stare at other people. Giving gifts is important, especially to those who are higher in the social hierarchy or are respected people. For example, if a mother-in law comes for a visit, she would expect a gift. The principle behind giving presents is that if God has been good to you, then you should be happy to spread that good fortune around.

Ivorian boys exhibiting their friendliness with big smiles.

DRESS

Ivorians place great importance on clothing. Their clothing can be divided into two types—traditional and casual dress. Traditional formal dress for men is pants and shirt underneath a long, embroidered robe that reaches to the ground. Their more casual clothes resemble Western-style pajamas. For women, traditional dress is also a long, embroidered robe. However, for daily wear a woman may put on a loose top and wrap a piece of colorful cloth around the waist for a skirt. Ivorian women also like to tuck their hair neatly under beautiful cloths with bright flower motifs. This is a practical and fashionable method to keep their hair out of the way while they work. Decorative fabrics are handmade in small cottage-type factories.

Below: **Women in traditional dress in Grand Bassam.**

Opposite: **A child enjoying every drop of his ice-cream, while hugging his toy car. Not every Ivorian child is fortunate enough to own toys.**

SOCIAL HIERARCHIES

From the 1960s to 1980s, there was a huge gap between the ruling elite and those who were ruled. The wealthy, urban, privileged minority received most of the benefits and had access to the country's resources. Political appointments were typically accompanied by land concessions in Abidjan. This resulted in a scarcity of land and high rents for everyone else. Cabinet ministers got monthly housing allowances and lived in relative luxury. Wealth and government service became closely linked. For those who lived in rural areas, secondary education and access to healthcare was nonexistent. Employment was a very significant indicator of social status. Government employees earned far more than the national average, while many people were unemployed in the rural sector. In general, the difference in the daily lives of the urban elite and the poor majority was huge.

The 1990s has seen some changes in this state of affairs. The middle class is expanding as the living standards of the low-wage workers rise. Opportunities for social mobility are slowly increasing. Unfortunately, for the very poor, living conditions have changed little. They remain alienated from the overall economic progress of the country.

LIFESTYLE

UNLIKE MOST OF AFRICA where rural life is predominant, in Côte d'Ivoire, about half the population lives in cities. More and more peasants are forced to find a living elsewhere, as deforestation makes the land too barren to grow crops. Increasingly, young people, mostly men, are drawn to the cities where they believe they will find a better standard of living. So they leave the countryside and head to the bustling urban centers. The most popular choices are Abidjan and Bouaké.

Unfortunately, these young people fail to realize that the transition from village life to a diverse, metropolitan environment can be extremely difficult. Unemployment in the cities has reached 25%, and many of the unemployed have turned to crime, causing the crime rate to increase at an alarming rate. But one thing is certain, whether Ivorians are living in the rural countryside or in the cities, the traditions of hospitality, family, and kinship are sustained.

Left: **An Ivorian man uses a computer at work. There are about 50,000 computers in Côte d'Ivoire, most of which belong to 3,000 registered companies.**

Opposite: **The wonder of these liana bridges is that they are built in a single night. No one knows how they are constructed because the Dan men who build them are sworn to secrecy, and no one is allowed to watch the process. The punishment for such violations is death.**

ROLE OF THE FAMILY

Above: **A young woman recuperating outside her house, while her sister looks on. There is no system of social security, so the family is the only source of support if one is unemployed, sick, or old.**

Opposite: **Ivorian women often have to carry their small children on their backs, while performing manual tasks like farming or fetching water from the river.**

In Côte d'Ivoire, the extended family is the basic social unit. The family is linked to a larger society through clans, called lineages, traced through male or female descent. An entire village is frequently from one single clan. Members of the same clan generally do not find a marriage partner within the group. Lineage ties enable people to live in harmony and foster a community spirit. They teach people history about their clan and enable them to cultivate a sense of social responsibility.

Every child born is a child of the entire village, and the child's success or failure is felt by everyone in the village. The responsibility to raise children and teach them social values belongs to everyone. This connection to others is of paramount importance. It is instilled at an early age, so that even if people leave the village, they will always act in the knowledge that they are a representative of their family and village. Thus, they should never bring disgrace on those still at home. This reinforces the important concept of community above self.

ROLE OF WOMEN

Traditionally a woman's role is to be a wife and mother. Boys are taught from an early age to always respect girls because one day the girls will be wives and mothers. Taking care of the family budget and children, particularly the girls, is the woman's responsibility. In Ivorian society, the relationship between a mother and her daughter is a very special one because they spend a lot of time together.

The woman is also expected to perform most of the less physical farming tasks, such as growing the vegetables and feeding the animals. For those women who can afford to attend school and complete their education, there are wider opportunities. An increasing number of women are employed in sectors of the economy such as medicine, business, and university teaching. Politically, women also have more say in the implementation of social policies.

The older, traditional woman may find it difficult to comprehend the choices that some modern Ivorian women have to make today, compared to the choices she had when she was their age. Some modern women can no longer accept their subordinate role in society, thus they openly challenge many conventions and traditions.

CHILDREN

Although elementary education is mandatory, the rule is not strictly enforced. Many children leave school at an early age, particularly girls and those living in rural areas. Children have to work on the farm as soon as they are old enough. For many, helping out takes priority over school.

By working beside their parents, children learn from an early age the values of their family and village. Girls are taught by their mothers, and boys predominantly talk to their fathers and other males. When the girls get married and leave home, the responsibility of taking care of the old folks at home falls on the sons. Rather than tell children what to do or what not to do, Ivorian parents get their message across with simple stories that have been handed down from generation to generation.

Ivorian parents love their children very much, so they take special care to instill in them the right values.

64

Separating rice grains from the husks. The average life expectancy for an Ivorian man is about 47 years.

IVORIAN MEN

An Ivorian man is brought up, first and foremost, to provide for his wife and family. The ability to do this well results in a higher social status for the individual. The continuing custom of polygamy depends on earning ability, because only a man who is doing well can afford to have more than one wife. A man will only look for another wife if he can provide for her. The woman and her family ensure that this is the case before agreeing to the marriage.

The last 20 years has seen many young men leaving their villages to seek better lives in the cities where there are more job opportunities, and they can earn more money. However, this migration has brought about many social problems. For many young men, life in these cities is very different from life at home. In a village it is perfectly natural to eat at any table and stay in any hut, but in the cities, one must pay for food and lodging. If the young man is poor, he will have to depend on relatives who live there.

A funeral procession for a woman who died of AIDS. Ivorians value life greatly. They believe that when a person dies, his death must be honored so that he can move on to the spiritual world peacefully. To do this, they perform funeral rites that may last up to a week.

LIFECYCLE EVENTS

Ceremonies, whether happy or sad, are an integral part of Ivorian society. Special events, such as births, weddings, and funerals, are given great attention. A birth is usually celebrated for one to two days. If the family is Christian, the child is baptised. Guests give the parents a gift, which is usually a small amount of money, and after the ceremony, everyone gathers for a feast.

Marriage is an important social institution, providing social cohesion in society and is an occasion for great celebration and joy. The marriage ceremony, attended only by relatives and the closest friends of the couple, is usually held at the mayor's office. The ceremony is the culmination of a week of activities including visits to relatives, feasts, and gifts.

For the ceremony, the bride decorates herself from head to foot. Each family brings wedding gifts of gold, silver, animals, food, and basic supplies for the couple to set up house together. The wedding guests are all invited to a feast with music and dancing.

STANDARD OF LIVING

Half the Ivorian population is urban, and many people live in slums in Abidjan and Bouaké. This is due to the high population growth and a steady economic decline since the 1980s. Urban centers such as Abidjan attract large numbers of rural migrants who come either as permanent settlers or as short-term workers. There are considerably more amenities in the cities of Abidjan and Bouaké, and many rich people live there.

But the daily life for the average young man looking for work and trying to survive can be hard. Government efforts to implement major structural reforms have led to disastrous results for many. The unemployment rate is very high in the cities. Although Côte d'Ivoire is making some progress in improving the overall standard of living, health services, and the literacy rate, it is moving at a very slow pace.

Few residents of the slums have access to electricity, a sewage system, or a clean water supply. Children defecate in streams filled with garbage, and women are forced to do their washing in the same streams.

More high-rise residential buildings are being constructed to cater to the Ivorians flocking to the cities.

67

URBAN LIVING

When a nuclear family living in the city is joined by their cousins and nephews from the countryside, their small, rented apartment becomes very crammed. The head of the household usually pays all the bills if he has a job and allows his cousins and nephews, or any relative in need, to stay for free at his house. Ivorians have long embraced their duty to care for their extended family. When their relatives approach them for help, they cannot turn them away because to do so is to risk isolation and scorn.

Those who have no relatives in the cities, mostly live in slum quarters. Shantytowns have rapidly sprung up around Abidjan in recent years. About 15% of Abidjan's population lives in these slums.

Thousands of middle-class Ivorians reside in expensive districts such as Deux Plateaux in Abidjan.

RURAL LIVING

Each village consists of several small settlements. The settlements include a number of mud huts with cone-shaped roofs made of palm leaves or thatch, or sometimes metal. The huts are grouped around a central compound, which serves as a meeting place. Every settlement is made up of several extended families, each of which is an economic unit. The Senufo live in villages of circular huts with unusual wooden doors.

A typical day for a rural family begins early. Rising at about 4 a.m., the men are the first to go to their land and start working. The women must first clean the house, get fires burning, and look after the children. Then they join their husbands later in the morning, taking care of the vegetable crops, such as peppers, potatoes, and peanuts. The men are responsible for clearing land so that yams, bananas, or other crops can be planted.

Farming is hard work. The farmers have to spend long hours under the scorching sun. The women return home at about 3 p.m. to tend to their children and to cook dinner. For the men, the day ends when the sun sets.

An aerial view of a Dioula village. The huts are usually built around a common area, where the villagers gather for meals and activities.

A young girl studies her textbook religiously. She is among the 31% of females who have the chance to pursue an education.

EDUCATION AND LITERACY

Education in Côte d'Ivoire is free through university level, and elementary education is compulsory. After four years of secondary education, students take exams. If they perform well, they get a certificate. After that, another three years is spent studying for the baccalaureate degree required to enter university. The National University of Côte d'Ivoire in Abidjan has a student body of about 21,000. A large number of students also study abroad.

During the 1970s, the educational system in Côte d'Ivoire was the envy of other African countries. The government had heavily subsidized education and even experimented with televised lessons, one of the few African nations to do so. However, the recession in the 1980s led to changes. Today, educational materials have to be paid for, and lack of funds for teachers and schools have taken a toll on education. Between 1980 and 1992, the percentage of those enrolled shrank from 79% to 69%. In the early 1990s, about 1.5 million students attended elementary schools, while 423,000 attended secondary and vocational schools.

The government is aware that a literacy rate of 64% and a system where a quarter of children, particularly girls and those living in rural parts, do not go to school is not acceptable. Although elementary education is compulsory, this requirement is not effectively enforced. Many children leave school after only a few years. Many parents prefer to send their boys for an education, a trend noticeable throughout the country but more pronounced in rural areas.

EDUCATIONAL PROGRAMS

Pierre Kipre, the nation's education minister, understands the important role of education to future development in a world where skilled workers are required. He has plans to provide more education in rural areas, as well as distance learning and apprenticeship programs. One difficulty, however, is that teachers are not paid very well and many job vacancies exist because the expanding private sector offers more financial rewards.

Consequently, the education minister has drawn up three literacy programs that give priority to women and children. Unveiled during the 1998 celebration of International Literacy Day in Abidjan and called "One Literate Woman, Three Children Educated," the first part of the five- year program is expected to help 25,000 women learn to read and write and get 75,000 rural children in school. In the second phase, the focus will be on girls, who are at present the most deprived of an education. The third phase aims to educate 10,000 women every year. Kipre said the goal is to increase the literacy rate to 85% as a whole by the year 2010. Some 70% of Ivorian women would be able to read and write by then.

HEALTH SERVICES AND CHALLENGES

With a ratio of 17,847 Ivorians to one doctor, health services, though improving, are still extremely inadequate. Public health programs are not provided enough funds, and health personnel are not given proper training.

Chronic malnutrition, resulting in stunted growth, is one of the most serious health problems for young children in the country. Children in rural areas are twice as likely to be underweight than those in the cities. As many as 35% of children three to 12 months old are underweight, and this figure is rapidly increasing. Another problem is river blindness, a disease transmitted by black flies.

These obstacles are an indication of the social and economic conditions the majority of Ivorians have to live with. In Côte d'Ivoire, only 41% of households have access to piped water. Poor people get their drinking water from surface water sources or open wells, both of which are often contaminated. Infants and children without access to tap water are at risk of poor hygiene and food contamination.

River blindness, a disease caused by a parasite, threatens more than 20,000 people in 21 villages in the district of Adzopé, about 50 miles (80 km) east of Abidjan. The principal carrier of the disease is the black fly, which breeds in the Komoé river. After the parasite enters the human body, it matures from larvae to worms. These worms migrate around the body and cause rashes and itching on the victim. When the worms enter the victim's eye, the victim will go blind. Most of those affected are less than 35 years old.

RELIGION

THERE ARE THREE MAJOR religions in Côte d'Ivoire. Some 23% of the people are Muslims while 12% are Christians—mostly Roman Catholics or Protestants. About 65% of the population practice traditional religions.

ISLAM

Islam, the second most widespread religion in Africa, was founded by the prophet Mohammed. Born in A.D. 570, he left Mecca in 610 and traveled, while preaching his divine revelations.

After Mohammed's death in 632, his followers collected his revelations and put them in a book called the Koran. This became the holy scripture of Islam. Another book was also compiled—the Hadith, which is a collection of all Mohammed's sayings. These were memorized and preserved by his companions. Muslims view the Hadith as an additional source of spiritual guidance, besides the Koran.

The constitution provides for freedom of religion. No religion is dominant, and no faith is officially favored. The government permits open religious practices and does not restrict religious teaching.

Opposite: **This post-Renaissance-style basilica, Our Lady of Peace, took three years to construct and is the largest church in the world after St. Peter's basilica in Rome, Italy, which took a century to build.**

Left: **Schoolchildren learn the Koran.**

There are five primary religious obligations that each Muslim must fulfill in his or her lifetime. They are called the "Five Pillars of Islam."

1. SHAHADAH ("sha-HAHD-ah") is the profession of faith. Muslims bear witness to the oneness of God by reciting the creed, "There is no deity but Allah" and "Mohammed is His servant and messenger." This simple, yet profound statement, expresses a Muslim's complete acceptance of, and total commitment to, the message of Islam.

2. SALAT ("sa-LAHT") is prayer. Muslims pray five times a day—at dawn, noon, midafternoon, sunset, and nightfall. Prayers link the worshipper to Allah. A prayer takes a few minutes to perform. There are no priests in Islam. Instead, a learned man chosen by his peers leads the prayers.

3. ZAKAT ("za-KAHT") means alms-giving, or giving up of one's surplus wealth. When Muslims give alms to the poor and needy, they must do it with sincerity and not expect something in return.

4. SAWM ("sa-AHM") is fasting. During the holy month of Ramadan, Muslims go without food and drink during daylight hours as an act of worship. Ramadan is the time when Muslims seek a richer perception of God. Fasting teaches them patience, unselfishness, moderation, willpower, discipline, a spirit of social belonging, unity, and brotherhood.

5. HAJJ ("HAHJ") means pilgrimage. It is the duty of every Muslim who is fit and can afford it to make at least one pilgrimage to Mecca. For some this involves a lifetime of savings. It is not unusual for families to save for years and then send only one member to represent the entire family.

Peace is the dominant theme in Islam. Peace with Allah, with one's soul, with the family and friends, and with all living creatures. To disturb the peace of anyone or any creature in any shape or form is strictly prohibited.

MOSQUES

Muslims worship Allah in a mosque. Early mosques resembled the courtyard of Mohammed's house, which was the place where the first Muslims gathered to listen to his sermons. Most mosques today are closed to non-Muslims because of an increased emphasis on the sanctity of the mosque. Muslims of all creeds are in theory free to enter all mosques, but in reality, a traveling Muslim will try to find a mosque that is used by people belonging to his own creed.

The design of the mosques developed from very simple to complex structures in a short time. The addition of minarets, or towers from which the calls to prayer are made, was inspired by other religious buildings. The idea of adorning the mosques was borrowed from churches. Over time, Muslims started to add rooms to the mosque. The rooms are used by people of different social classes. Devout Muslims often live in the mosque. When entering the mosque, a person has to take off his shoes. Entering the mosque has to be done with the right foot first, while uttering blessings to Mohammed and his family. A person inside the mosque has to talk softly so that he does not disturb the people who are praying.

Women are not prevented from entering mosques by the Islamic faith, but for a long time, in practice, they have not been welcomed. Mosques can be closed to women, either by local rules or by habit.

Although it is considered more meritorious to pray in the mosque with other people, a Muslim may pray almost anywhere, such as in the fields, in offices, factories, or universities. However, the Friday prayer or sermon is considered to be compulsory for all male Muslims.

A mud mosque in Ferkéssédougou. Wooden stakes help to support the earthen walls.

Opposite: **The building of St. Paul's Cathedral indicates a shift towards modern architectural styles.**

CHRISTIANITY

Christianity, Africa's most widespread religion, was introduced to northern Africa in the first century A.D. By the fourth century A.D., it had spread to other parts of Africa. Christianity has survived in some countries, but in many others, it has been replaced by Islam. Today, in Côte d'Ivoire, Christianity exists, and both Catholic and Protestant groups can be found.

Roman Catholicism in Côte d'Ivoire was reintroduced by French missionaries during the colonial period, particularly among the Agni people. It is still most prevalent among them today. In general, Roman Catholicism is practiced by the middle class and urban south. Villages adopt certain patron saints and honor them on secular and religious holidays. The first African Roman Catholic mission was established in 1895, and the first African priest ordained in 1934. In the 1980s the church started seminaries and schools throughout the country, and a large cathedral, St. Paul's Cathedral, was built in Abidjan. In 1990 the former president, Houphouët-Boigny, funded the building of a basilica, Our Lady of Peace.

PLACES OF WORSHIP

OUR LADY OF PEACE, situated in Houphouët-Boigny's birthplace, Yamoussoukro, is a massive 7.4-acre (3-hectare) plaza with a marble Roman-style entrance. It cost US$400 million to build, and the maintenance costs are an annual US$1.5 million. With a massive cross on top, it claims to be the tallest church in the world. In September 1990 Pope John Paul II visited Côte d'Ivoire for the third time and consecrated the basilica. Since then it has been visited by more than two million people and is becoming a pilgrimage stop for many Catholics around the world.

The area of Our Lady of Peace is enormous—it can hold 300,000 people. The cathedral has 36 beautiful stained-glass windows, the glass all hand-blown in France. The figures depicted in the windows are all Caucasian except for one sole black pilgrim who resembles Houphouët-Boigny. He is shown kneeling at the feet of Christ.

ST. PAUL'S CATHEDRAL is a modern and attractive cathedral with a big tower that affords a great view of the city of Abidjan. It was designed by an Italian and consecrated by the Pope in 1985.

About 120,000 Ivorians were personally baptized by William Harris.

HARRISM

This is the largest and oldest Protestant religion in the country. Founded in 1914 by a Liberian, William Harris, Harrism is considered more an African religion than a Western one taught by white missionaries. Traveling through Ghana and Côte d'Ivoire, Harris led a simple life. He attracted followers by preaching against adultery, theft, and lying, and condemning excessive wealth. Harris viewed the traditional belief in the power of charms against evil as ignorance. His style of Christianity was open to all people, and he succeeded partly because he was African and partly because he showed no sexual discrimination. Thus women, as well as men, converted to Harrism. Earlier Christian missionaries had not understood the importance of matrilineal descent in Ivorian society.

Although the teachings and beliefs of Harrism were not really in opposition to the colonial authorities, in 1915, a nervous French governor asked Harris to leave. This revitalized his church tremendously, and many small Harrist churches sprung up along the coast. By 1925 Methodist missionaries were continuing his work among the lagoon people of the southwest, and Harrism became recognized as a branch of Methodism.

TRADITIONAL RELIGIONS

The majority of Ivorians practice traditional religions involving ancestral worship. Each ethnic group has its own distinctive religious practices, but some elements are common to all. All traditional religions are animistic, which means that people believe everything has a soul. They also accept the notions of a supreme being and reincarnation. Besides the Creator, there are numerous lesser gods that Ivorians pray to for good health, bountiful harvests, and numerous children, and whom they honor in village celebrations. In addition, they worship ancestral spirits.

Ancestral spirits are those members of the family or lineage who have died and transformed into spirits. They remain in constant contact with the living. Through various rituals, the living seek their blessings and protection. The principal role of the ancestral spirits is to protect the tribe. The ancestral spirits are also the real owners of the land—the villagers cannot sell it or they would incur their wrath. Magic is also commonly practiced in traditional rituals. Good magic keeps evil spirits away, and

Amulets, charms, and magical medicines on sale in the Bouaké market.

A roadside memorial built to honor a dead Ivorian.

medicine men dispense charms, tell fortunes, and give advice on how to avoid danger. They also bless *grisgris* ("GREE-gree"), which are charmed necklaces that ward off specific evils. If the *grisgris* has not been blessed by the medicine man, it will not protect the person wearing it.

The Senufo religious leaders, or *marabous* ("MAR-e-boo"), officiate at ceremonies, honor the gods, and advise people on how to cope with their problems. Sometimes they act as doctors, because many illnesses are thought to have spiritual causes.

The Agni and Baule have a single god or creator figure, Nyame, and a number of subordinate gods who inhabit trees, water, and animals. Below them are lesser deities whose power is invoked through protective charms. The ancestral spirits who affect the people's daily lives are always in contact with the living and can directly influence a person's fortunes in his present life. Thus it is important for the living to ask for their blessings and protection through various ceremonies. Ancestral spirits are always consulted, sometimes even offered food and drink. Failure to perform such rites makes the spirits angry and can result in misfortune.

The Kru believe in a second god besides the Creator. This god is a devil who works against the Creator and results in humans having a balance of good and evil within themselves. The crux is to maintain this balance.

The Dioula believe that God created the world and four sets of twins. These twins were commanded to populate earth and to teach their children to grow crops.

The Lobi think of divination as a means of determining death, disease, or any misfortune. Diviners act like counselors, not predicting the future but suggesting some action to help a person cope with their problems.

The Kulango believe in a god who is not worshipped but is addressed in association with "mother earth." The earth god is the god of the whole tribe. During disasters or hard times, the Kulango pray to the spirits of their ancestors and make offerings of mashed yams.

A BLEND OF THE THREE RELIGIONS

Over the centuries, both Christian and Islamic rites and beliefs have been incorporated into tribal religions. New religious movements that contain elements from the different religions have also been formed. Led by individual prophets, these separatist groups mix beliefs from different sources to help people deal with daily life. Most popular among minority groups trying to resist domination by others, such religions are evolving and finding a place among Ivorians. For example, although many of the Agni have remained Roman Catholic, their neighbors, the Baule, have followed the new prophets who promise good fortune to those who revere them.

A Muslim imam in the town of Niofouin. Niofouin is famous for its blend of animist and Muslim religions.

LANGUAGE

THE OFFICIAL NATIONAL LANGUAGE of Côte d'Ivoire is French, a legacy of the earlier colonial administration. Educated Ivorians are bilingual, speaking French and their mother tongue, which is the language of their village and ethnic group. With 60 different ethnic groups, this means that there are as many languages spoken in the country.

SPOKEN LANGUAGES

The 60 languages of Côte d'Ivoire are all grouped under the Niger-Congo language family, a family of languages widely spoken in west, central, and south Africa. Languages of the Niger-Congo family are called tone languages because tones serve phonetically to distinguish the meanings of words. Different words are distinguished merely by changes in the pitch of a single syllable. These different pitches are crucial to understanding

Some African languages are spoken by relatively few people. For example, the Ega language is spoken by only 290 people.

Opposite: **A hairdresser's sign showing different trendy hairstyles.**

Left: **A traditional medicine man displays the effects of his healing formulas on the posters behind him.**

A couple enjoy a drink and a conversation at a French café.

exactly what is said. In such cases, one word may have a number of different meanings depending upon which syllable is intoned higher or given more stress.

There are four branches of the Niger-Congo family in Côte d'Ivoire— the Kwa, the Mande, the Kru, and the Gur languages. The Kwa branch consists of the Baule language, which is spoken by over two million people. The Abron and Agni languages also belong to this group. The Mande branch includes the Dioula language, spoken by over a million people. The Dan language belongs to the Mande branch and has existed for 5,000 years. It is considered the oldest offshoot of the family. The Kru branch consists of the Kru language. The Gur branch refers to the Senufo language, which is spoken by over one million people. The Lobi and Kulango languages are some of the languages that belong to the Gur branch. Each of these languages has many dialects. Thus people living in different regions have different pronunciations of the same words. For example, the Dioula language has 22 dialects.

FRENCH

French belongs to the Indo-European language family. It is taught in school, so anyone who can afford to go to school will be able to speak and write French. Although the language was imposed on the Ivorians during colonial days and is not a native language, it provides people with a common communication tool. Without French, problems would arise when people try to converse in 60 different languages. It would be impossible to choose any local language as the official one because not more than a 10th of the population can understand any single native language.

Unlike English, French has no stress. It has a musical inflection that runs throughout a sentence, not just on individual words. When speaking French, an equal stress is applied on all the syllables, although there are occasions when the last syllable has a lighter stress. Two common French words are *bonjour* ("BON-zhoor"), which means "good morning," and *au revoir* ("ORE-re-voir"), which means "goodbye."

ORAL TRADITIONS

Ivorian cultural expression remains very distinct today, particularly in its oral forms. Although writing traditions exist, Ivorians are primarily a vocal people, as are most Africans. Throughout history, Ivorians have regarded the oral language as a potent force. All the people share and value this heritage. In a country where many ethnic languages coexist and a colonial language was imposed on everyone, it requires much effort to preserve a written literature for each ethnic language. Thus it was necessary to convey African stories and folklore through an oral tradition.

MEDIA

There are 11 daily newspapers, all in French. Four of them are more widely read than the rest. They include *Fraternité Matin*, *Le Jour*, *La Nouvelle République*, and *La Voie*. Several other newspapers are printed weekly.

The government owns two daily newspapers, two major radio stations, and the only two television channels in Côte d'Ivoire. Only the government

GRIOTS AS ORAL HISTORIANS

Traditional *griots* ("GREE-ohs") are either attached to leading households in African societies or serve as freelance poets. In either role, they exercise their vast knowledge of history, language, and the lineage of their patrons by praise singing, commentary, and instrumental accompaniment. *Griots* are historians, praise singers, and musical entertainers. Yet none of these descriptions quite captures their unique status in Dioula society. They are educated and wise, and they use their detailed knowledge of history to shed light on present-day dilemmas. In the past, *griots* tutored princes and gave council to kings. Now, a rich Dioula family employs their own *griot* to advise them and help them negotiate matters with other families. *Griots* arrange marriages and mediate disputes, always relying on their understanding of each family's history.

radio and television stations are broadcast nationwide. Radio Abidjan broadcasts in some of the main languages such as Dioula and Baule. There are four radio stations that are not under government control. Apart from the two national television stations, there is a private television subscription service, Canal Horizon.

While the independent stations have control over their editorial content, the government exercises considerable influence over the media to promote government policies. Much of the news is devoted to the activities of the president, the government, and the PDCI.

The government-owned newspapers rarely have any policy criticisms in their reports. Despite significant restrictions, independent and opposition newspapers frequently voice their disapproval of government actions. It is a crime to defame the president, prime minister, foreign chiefs of state or their diplomatic representatives, or state institutions. In 1991 a new commission was set up to enforce laws against publishing material "undermining the reputation of the nation or defaming institutions of the State." In August 1995 the editor of the daily paper *Le Populaire* was arrested after the publication of an article alleging abuse of power by a public prosecutor. The article included a photo of an internal document, and the editor was charged with possession of a controlled government document. In the same year, three opposition party journalists were convicted for publishing an article attributing the poor performance of an Ivorian soccer team to the president's presence at the international match. With the threat of a jail sentence, journalists are extremely careful what they write.

The Television Tower in Bouaké transmits programs to three million television sets in the country.

ARTS

IVORIAN ART IS UNIQUE and is of great significance throughout the country. The family and ethnic groups are such crucial parts of life that all expressions of art serve to reinforce existing religious and social patterns.

Sculpture, masks, pottery, decorative textiles, and jewelry are examples of what Ivorian artists can create. The most popular materials used include wood, fiber, ivory, clay, earth, and stone. There is a practical purpose behind every piece of traditional Ivorian art, usually to do with religious matters, or seeking health, village harmony, and successful harvests.

THE INDIGENOUS CULTURE

Before Europeans arrived, a lot of cultural influences from other parts of Africa spread through Côte d'Ivoire as a result of the Saharan trade routes. When the French came, they brought along their culture. Modern Ivorians are greatly influenced by European culture, sometimes to the extent of

Traditional art typically shows women as mothers nursing their children. Men are usually presented as community leaders and fighters.

Opposite: **Carved wooden statues of the Baule tribe. These "dream lover" statues represent spiritual spouses in the netherworld. Individuals who have marital or childbearing problems will sleep alone with these statues for one night a week to commune with the spirits.**

Left: **Buying fabrics in a textile market in Abidjan.**

89

rejecting traditional ones. Fortunately, with the rise in African nationalism, a cultural revival is occurring in all African countries. Côte d'Ivoire is no exception. The government encourages and provides support to dance troupes, music groups, artists, writers, and even the museum. Thus, the indigenous culture remains strong.

The art of Côte d'Ivoire is among the best in West Africa and is distinct to each ethnic group. Three groups, the Baule, Dan, and Senufo, stand out from the rest. A common Dan carving is that of a large spoon for serving rice. These spoons typically have two legs resembling human legs. The Senufo carve ornate doors to protect their community's food supplies. The Baule sculpt vessels for oracular purposes.

MASKS AND STATUES

Masks and statues are used during dances, masquerades, and religious ceremonies. They are carved out of a single block of wood and decorated with clay, shells, beads, ivory, or feathers.

An Ivorian statue on display in the national museum.

Ivorian art, like all African art, is rooted in ancestor worship. A mask represents the bond between a people and their ancestors and is valued for the tradition it represents. The belief is that both man and animal are part of the natural order, and that man should experience a oneness with all things in the natural world. Since all natural elements contain an inner energy, the masks and statues collect this energy from the dead. They are "spirit traps," used to control spirits and benefit the living. Masks are also used to illustrate gender roles in interesting ways.

DIFFERENT TYPES OF MASKS

During the construction of an ancestral mask, sculptors carve facial and body features differently from those on masks used for entertainment. They adopt communally approved artistic codes, such as the use of white as the color of death or the rendering of animal forms to reinforce the representation of the mask. For example, the lion signifies strength, the spider shows prudence, and horns means the moon and fertility.

The most common Dan mask is a human face, slightly abstract but with realistic features, a smooth surface, everted lips, slit or large circular eyeholes, and a calm expression. The slit-eyed ones are used to keep women from seeing uncircumcised boys during their initiation into adulthood. Traditionally used in commemorative ceremonies, Baule facial masks are very realistic and tend to portray individuals who can be easily recognized by their facial marks or hairstyles.

Above: **The wisdom mask, known as Nanh-Sohou, is considered the father of masks. As such, it is rarely seen, only during funerals of important people and in the presence of many other masks.**

Left: This modern masquerade, with masks representing interesting characters such as a clown, demonstrates the creativity and skill of the Ivorlans.

The masks and figures made by the Senufo people are used in ceremonies held to honor village life. Senufo masks are highly stylized—the most famous is the "fire spitter" helmet mask, which is a combination of the antelope, wart hog, and hyena. Another is the wart hog mask, made to get rid of evil spirits. Hornbill figures, in a variety of sizes and styles, are important because the hornbill was the mythological founder of the Senufo people and a symbol of fertility.

One figure in particular has a long, hooked beak touching a protruding stomach, symbolizing the continuation of life to future generations. Hornbills are considered admirable because they mate for life and share in the raising of the young. The figures are worn on the head during dances and processions.

Dance masks are used in village masquerades at the end of harvest festivities. Totemic masks, such as the elephant mask representing the totem of its wearer, appear first. The Gu mask, representing a beautiful woman, is a principal mask in the masquerade. Portrait masks are the last to be seen. They are portraits of individuals representing an ideal value. An example is a face with eyes downcast and lips closed, which shows respect and composure.

INTERWEAVING MASKS, MUSIC, AND DANCE

Ivorian traditions have unified the masquerade, music, and dance as a continuation of creation and life. In the context of the masquerade, the mask has a deep cultural significance. It provides a visual representation of the invisible spirits, and the masquerade often becomes the manner in which the divine or ancestral spirits intervene from behind the masks.

The musician's role is to invoke the spirit to enter the masquerader, after which the mask and dancer are considered sacred and not to be desecrated. During the masquerade, the masked dancer is granted symbolic status and any comments that they make are believed to be coming from the particular ancestor or god that is now in possession of their body. In such a ritual, the supernatural becomes an actual presence, ready to intervene in the affairs of the living. Alternatively the occasion may be used to subtly convey messages and criticisms to members of the community, which if delivered in a different context, would invoke anger and hostility.

The musical instrument is crucial in reinforcing the idea that external forces are lurking. As a rule, instruments are made according to the tastes and habits of the musician. The tuning of these instruments is subject to the language patterns of the musician's mother tongue, as are the rhythms generated when they are played. The resonating space within the completed instrument is believed to give fullness to the ancestral voices, and it is the musician's performance on particular instruments that enables the ancestors to present themselves through the body of the dancers.

A dancer's body is thus considered an instrument that can be played by a skilled musician. The dancer, who is knowledgeable in the language of the music, makes certain audible or physical responses to particular sounds and rhythms, thereby translating these sounds into a dialogue.

Before constructing an instrument, the maker has to present offerings in a ritual to honor the ancestral spirits who are believed to reside in the instrument.

Opposite: **A young Dan boy performs a tribal dance.**

To the Ivorians, music is an integral part of life, and it is said that each of them has a rhythm to which they dance, or alternatively— since words are embedded in these rhythms—a call to which they respond.

TRADITIONAL MUSIC

The country's traditional music is characterized by a series of melodies and rhythms occurring in harmony. It may seem monotonous to some people, but in fact, African rhythms contain influences from Western popular music such as jazz, blues, and rock.

Music is used to transmit knowledge and values and for celebrating communal and personal events. Stages of a person's life are marked with music specific to adolescent initiation rites, weddings, ancestral ceremonies, and funerals. There are different kinds of music for women, men, young people, and hunters.

Traditional music includes the use of a wide variety of instruments that are made with local materials. Drums are among the most popular instruments used. They come in a number of shapes, such as cylindrical, kettle, and hourglass. Several materials, such as wood, gourds, and clay, are used to construct drum bodies. Membranes are made from the skins of reptiles, cattle, goats, and other animals.

DRUM ENSEMBLES

Important types of drums include drum-chimes in which a set of drums tuned to a scale is mounted in a frame and played by a team of drummers; friction drums, in which a sound is produced by rubbing the membrane; and the hourglass-shaped tension drum.

Drum ensembles consisting of three to five musicians who play connecting patterns are common. In the ensemble, each drummer uses a special method of striking the drum head to produce varying pitches to distinguish the drum from all the others. Such ensembles often include rattles and an iron bell, which is struck with a stick to produce a repeated pattern called a timeline.

Ivorian drummers play a critical role in ceremonies during which the gods enter the bodies of devotees. The drummer must know scores of specific rhythms for particular gods and be responsible throughout the performance for monitoring the flow of supernatural power.

Other important percussion instruments include clap sticks, bells, rattles, gourds and claypots, xylophones, and the lamellaphone. The latter is a series of metal or bamboo strips mounted on a board. It is held in the hands or on the player's lap, and the free ends of the strips are plucked with the thumbs. String instruments include the musical bow, lute, and harp. The flute, whistle, oboe, and trumpet are the wind instruments. Flutes are made from bamboo, reeds, wood, clay, or bones. Trumpets are made from corn stems from the savanna areas with a reed cut from the surface of the stem at one end.

Historically, traditional music has been the prerogative of one social group, the *griot*. They played a crucial role as historians in the kingdoms that developed from the 10th century to the 20th century across Africa as a whole and Côte d'Ivoire in particular. At sometime, *griots* became the official musicians of society. They used only instruments they could make themselves, with local materials such as gourds, animal skins, and horns.

Traditional musicians performing with the *balafon* (left), the Ivorian xylophone, and the cylindrical calabash (right), a stringed instrument. The long wooden neck of the calabash keeps the leather strings in place.

The *griot's* ancient art is still practiced today, though some say it has declined under the pressures of modern society. Today, families generally cannot afford their own private *griot*, so the musicians move from family to family, performing at weddings and baptisms, entertaining and praising the guests. One need only turn on the radio or the television, or go to a music festival to experience their enduring power.

Walking along a residential street, a traditional wedding may be encountered. A crowd of nicely dressed men and women will be gathered in the dirt street around a group of musicians playing through cranked-up amplifiers. There may be guitars, *balafon* ("BAH-lah-fon," a wooden xylophone), or *kora* ("KOH-rah," a 21-string cross between a harp and a lute), all weaving a web of intricate melodies. Leading the entertainment will be a female *griot* singer in a fabulous, embroidered gown, singing her heart out. *Griots* sing in loud, proud voices full of the grandeur of their history. Their vocal styles reflect the influence of Islam on the music of the savanna region. The great majority of these beloved and respected vocalists are women. Guests will circulate before her, and if she praises them by name, they will give her money.

POPULAR MUSIC

Ivorian popular music is an amazing blend of African, European, American, and Middle Eastern traditions. It was created by those who came to this country during the 20th century. Ballads were introduced at that time, and sailors from all over the world introduced the Ivorians to accordions and string instruments such as guitars. The subsequent development of popular music has been strongly influenced by the electronic mass media and the growing popularity of African music in the international music scene in the late 20th century.

Dancing during a wed-
ding ceremony in Grand
Bassam.

TRADITIONAL DANCE

Dance is as varied in style and function as music. Dancing is associated
with both sacred and secular events, and it plays a crucial role in education,
work, entertainment, politics, and religious ritual. Common dance patterns
include team dances using formations; group dances that allow individuals
to display their skills; and solo dances, often performed by a professional
entertainer. Body postures in Ivorian dance are typically earth-oriented
movements in which the performer bends the knees and inclines the torso
forward from the hips.

Some of the well-known dances include the N'Goron dance, a graceful
initiation dance by young Senufo girls wearing only grass skirts and shell
and feather headdresses; and the panther dance, which illustrates the
courage, agility, and strength of the Senufo peasant in mastering a hostile
environment. It is usually performed when boys return from the Poro
training sessions. Other dances are the Koutouba and Kouroubissi dances,
performed by Malinke women during the week before Ramadan.

TEXTILES

The Ivorians view textiles and the decorative arts used in textiles as works of art and social communication that cannot be minimized. In particular the art of making korhogo cloth is a tradition that is handed down from one generation to another. Korhogo cloth is a handpainted fabric woven by Senufo weavers. The intricate symbols and patterns drawn on the cloth are evidence of their skill in and mastery of the traditional art of making textiles. The cloth is recognizable by the bold figures, usually dark brown or black, painted on plain cotton material, usually white.

Korhogo craftsman cooperate in an organized manner. Cotton spinning and dyeing are done by women and the weaving is handled by men. Handpainting on the cloth is done with a mixture extracted from the bark and leaves of a shrub. It is used to draw mostly geometric figures and animal motifs such as chickens, lizards, and snakes. Originally the decorated material was used by those being initiated and by hunters and dancers.

Handpainting a cloth requires an extremely steady hand and a lot of patience. Artisans like the one above have gone through extensive training starting when they were young.

JEWELRY

Jewelry is important to both Ivorian men and women. There are many types of jewelry. Beads are used to create objects that represent spiritual values, and such objects play major roles in community events like birth, marriage, and death. Most common are the glass beads worn by village chiefs and elders as a sign of power and wealth. Other materials used for making beads include coral, shells, silver, and gold. Gold and silver are precious and are sold by the gram. The necklaces that ward off evil are characterized by protective symbolism and come in various designs. Some incorporate circle designs or fertility designs for both sexes, while others may represent animal tracks showing power and cunning. Rings, earrings, and bracelets also vary in style.

LITERARY ARTS

Côte d'Ivoire's most famous and prolific writer is Bernard Dadié, whose work has been widely translated. One of his novels, *Climbié* (1971), is an autobiographical account of a childhood journey to France. Other translated works include *The Black Cloth* and *The City Where No One Dies*. Other well-known national novelists include Aké Loba and Ahmadou Kourouma. The former is best known for *Kocoumbo*, an autobiographical novel of an African suffering the effects of being uprooted and poverty-stricken in Paris who is drawn toward militant communism. Kourouma's hit novel, *The Suns of Independence*, tells the story of a village chief deposed after independence, losing his subjects and having to adjust to a different life.

Shell headdresses are popular with rural women because they believe that shells can keep evil away.

99

LEISURE

FOR THE MAJORITY of the Ivorians who work hard all year, the Western concept of leisure is somewhat alien. Rather than resting and relaxing during their free time, the Ivorians, after finishing their chores, happily participate in the many communal events and celebrations of village life. The times that are not filled with activity are usually spent with those of the same sex, playing boardgames, talking, and exchanging ideas. Conveying ideas through storytelling is an enjoyable experience for all involved. For those people who live and work in the towns and cities, there might be more free time. The sandy beaches of Grand Bassam are favorite weekend retreats for them.

Sports are a popular pastime for everyone in Côte d'Ivoire, whether they are active players or simply observers. Many often gather for a game when their chores are done. Children are also strongly encouraged to take up sports to build up their stamina and lead healthy lifestyles.

Not all children can afford to buy toys and play arcade games *(left)*. Many rural children have to resort to making their own playthings. These children *(opposite)* proudly show off their handmade wooden toys.

TRADITIONAL GAMES

Similar to backgammon, the game of *awale* ("a-WA-lay") is an intellectual pastime enjoyed by Ivorians of all ages. It can be played by two people or by teams of more people. The rules are not difficult, but playing the game well takes a lot of practice. The *awale* board is rectangular, about 20 inches (50 cm) long, with two rows of six cups each. Game pieces are 48 peas. There are several versions of the game played by the different ethnic groups, but certain features are common in all versions.

To start the game, four peas are placed in each cup. The first player starts by picking up all the peas from any cup on his/her side of the board and dropping them one at a time in each consecutive cup to the right, counterclockwise. A person scores by capturing peas, and the winner is the one who captures the most peas. A person captures peas only when the last pea dropped falls in a cup on the opponent's side that contains only one or two peas. When that happens, the player picks up all the peas in that cup and stores them for counting at the end of the game.

STORYTELLING

Stories help people identify who they are in relation to others and often aid the understanding of a culture. Ivorian storytelling is full of wisdom, experience, and the teachings of a people who depended on oral tradition to pass stories from one generation to another. These stories are a powerful educational tool because they often teach the listeners some important lessons about traditional values and life. Accompanied by music and sometimes dance, the stories can be about people, animals, or spirits, whether they are good or evil. The stories introduce their listeners to a world of knowledge, mystery, and magic that appeals to their emotions. Children love to listen to the stories their elders tell them. They often gather in the communal area for some storytelling when the elders are free.

Even though some of these stories can now be found in books, Ivorian parents still prefer to relate them directly to their children because these storytelling sessions can enhance their parent-child ties.

AN IVORIAN TALE

One popular tale tells of a girl who gets lost in the woods and encounters a dirty and scruffy old woman. The old woman asks the girl to help clean her. The kindhearted girl agrees and is rewarded with a bowl that she is told to take home. The girl takes the bowl home and carefully places it in the house. The next day when she wakes up, the house is full of gold and silver! When the other villagers see this, they are very jealous. One woman instructs her daughter to go to the woods and find this old woman.

The girl reluctantly does as she is told. When she meets the old woman, she refuses to help her. The old woman gives the girl three bowls anyway and tells her to throw the biggest one away, followed by the medium one. The small bowl is to be taken home. However, this greedy girl throws away the little one first, then the middle one, and takes the large one home. She thinks that the biggest bowl must contain the greatest amount of gold. The next day, instead of riches, she wakes up to find the house infested with disease, poverty, and unhappiness.

SPORTS

Rugby is a popular sport in Côte d'Ivoire. There is a national team, and though relatively inexperienced, they participate in the World Cup. Basketball and softball are also commonly played. The latter has a strong association to represent its interests in Abidjan. Golf can be played as both Abidjan and Yamoussoukro have two good courses with grass greens. Because golf is such an expensive sport, it is mostly limited to tourists or businessmen. Locals are more likely to be seen on the less desirable green sand course. Surfing, for those who can afford the expensive equipment, is possible at the beaches. Most people opt to swim in pools found at the big hotels and in some of the main cities, as strong currents along the coast make swimming there dangerous.

Soccer is the nation's favorite sport. There are matches to watch every Sunday in the major cities. Unofficial games are always being played on the beach, in the streets, or at the university or municipal stadium. From an early age, boys are encouraged to take up the sport. The Ivorians are proud of their national soccer team. National pride swells whenever the team performs well in international tournaments. There are several soccer clubs in the country.

OTHER ENTERTAINMENT

For adults, dancing is very popular. There are many places to go dancing, and dancing to a live African band is possible every night except on Sundays for as little as a US$6 entrance fee. Discotheques are the favorite entertainment spot for younger people. On weekends, these places become very crowded. Movie theaters attract a large audience too, with three to four screenings a day in big cities such as Yamoussoukro and Bouaké. Most city people can afford this cheap entertainment.

There is a skating rink in the biggest hotel in Abidjan, Hotel Ivoire, and the rink is marketed as the only one in the whole of West Africa. However, it is an expensive recreation restricted to urban teenagers who can afford to pay the high price. In the capital, horseback riding is a popular pastime. Several riding clubs organize excursions to the forests and seaside.

Opposite: **Ivorians enjoy a game of basketball.**

Left: **A young boy skates with ease and style.**

FESTIVALS

IVORIANS CELEBRATE many festivals throughout the year, most of which are closely tied to their religion. These festivals are usually a time to commemorate their Christian, Islamic, or traditional gods. Besides religious occasions, secular holidays also form a big part of the local festivities scene.

CHRISTIAN HOLIDAYS

The Ivorians celebrate several Roman Catholic holidays. Easter, which celebrates the resurrection of Jesus Christ, is usually in April. Ascension Day, the ascension of Jesus Christ to heaven on the 40th day after the resurrection, is celebrated in May. Whit Sunday falls on the seventh Sunday after Easter. This festival commemorates the descent of the Holy Spirit on the day of Pentecost. Assumption Day, the reception of Our Lady into heaven, is in August. All Saints' Day on November 1 honors loved ones who have died. Christmas Day celebrates the birth of Jesus Christ.

Opposite: **Dan stilt dancers rest against a rooftop after a performance. Some of their stilts can be as high as 10 feet (3 m).**

Left: **Girls selling fruit in Abidjan. Every Christmas, the city brightens up with Christmas lights and festive decorations.**

A meat stall in the market. The price of sheep increases by 50% before Eid al-Adha. People will try to find the money to buy one as it is too embarrassing to go without on this holiday.

MUSLIM CELEBRATIONS

The Muslims celebrate Ramadan, which is the ninth month of the Islamic calendar. During the month of Ramadan, Muslims fast between sunrise and sunset. According to the fourth pillar of Islam, fasting brings one closer to Allah. The discipline of fasting reminds Muslims of people who are deprived of basic necessities and the sufferings of less fortunate people. It also encourages Muslims to show sympathy and kindness toward these people.

Ramadan ends with a huge feast, called the Feast of Breaking the Fast or Eid al-Fitr, which follows the sighting of the new moon. It is a joyous occasion when everyone prays together, visits friends and relatives, exchanges gifts, and eats lots of good food. In many ways it is similar to the spirit of Thanksgiving Day. On Eid al-Fitr Muslims show thanks for health, strength, and the opportunities in life given to them by Allah. Although the celebration lasts for two to 10 days, depending on the region, the main activities occur on the first day.

The festival begins with a special prayer performed in a mosque. After the prayer, people greet each other warmly and give presents to the children. Then they visit relatives and friends, and everyone asks for forgiveness for any wrongdoings in the previous year.

The Feast of the Sacrifice, Eid al-Adha, starts on the 10th day of the last month of the Islamic calendar. This is also the month of pilgrimage to Mecca. The feast is especially meaningful to those who have made the pilgrimage. On that morning, Muslims assemble at the communal place of prayer, usually an open field, to pray together. After prayers, the head of each household sacrifices a sheep, a camel, or an ox for his family.

The person faces Mecca and calls out the names of the persons on whose behalf the sacrifice is being made. Then he says the words, "In the name of Allah who is the Almighty," and in one stroke, cuts the throat of the animal with a very sharp knife. The sacrificed animal is divided into three portions—one for the family, the second for relatives and friends, and the third share for the poor and needy.

During the Eid, prayers are usually performed by the whole Muslim community.

The jugglers dance—the girls' faces, decorated with white paste, are perfectly still as they pirouette and somersault with great skill and flexibility.

TRADITIONAL FESTIVALS

THE FESTIVAL OF MASKS, or Fêtes des Masques, is celebrated annually by the Dan people. It takes place in the Man villages each February. Each village in Man uses several masks and dances for this festival. Two famous dances are the stilt dance and the jugglers dance.

The stilt dance is a unique dance performed by a group of young, masked Dan men. During their three to five years of training, the dancers are instructed not to tell anyone, not even their wives, what they are doing. After their training, they can communicate with the spirits, who direct the dancers' complex acrobatic stunts during the dance.

Every village in the west has its own version of the jugglers dance. Typically, a drumroll introduces the performers. This is followed with a dance by the guardian mask to exorcise evil spirits. Then young men, armed with sharp daggers, juggle 10-year-old girls in the air and catch them, while holding the daggers but without ever cutting them. The girls wear skirts made of grass and headdresses decorated with cowrie shells.

THE FEAST OF DIPRI, or Fête du Dipri, takes place in April in Gomon, 62 miles (100 km) northwest of Abidjan. This is the home of the Abidji, the local ethnic group. The festive action starts around midnight, although the entire village has been awake for some time within the safety of their huts. Only naked women and children sneak out of their huts to carry out nocturnal rites to rid the village of evil spells. Before sunrise, the chief appears, calling out to his people, "Chase out the evil."

The entire village then emerges from their homes screaming out these same words. Drums pound, and the villagers slip into trances. Bodies squirm in the dust, people's eyes roll up into their sockets, and young people beat themselves and the ground with sticks. The frenzy continues until noon when the magic exercises begin. These exercises are initiation rituals for the Abidji. With sharp daggers, the initiates cut their stomachs. The men are not hurt as their wounds heal quickly after being smeared with a balm prepared by medicine men. No one may enter the village of Gomon on the festival day itself.

These participants are oblivious to their surroundings because they are said to be possessed by spirits. There is a story behind the feast of Dipri. In the early 20th century, there was a terrible famine in that region. A genie advised the chieftain of the land to cut his son, Bidyo, into many pieces and bury them. To save his people, he followed the genie's advice. To his surprise, yams started sprouting from the spot where his son was buried. So the feast of Dipri is held every April to commemorate Bidyo's sacrifice.

A mask of the Dan tribe. It can be easily identified by the almond-shaped eyes and the emotionless face.

YAM FESTIVALS are celebrated at the beginning and end of harvests with music, dances, and masquerades. The yam is such an integral part of the people's diet that a good harvest makes a great difference to their lives. Therefore, the Ivorians take this opportunity to honor the spirits and ancestors who protect their crops, and to ensure their good graces.

For the Agni and Baule people, the yam festival starts with the *anaya* ("a-NAI-ya"), a food offering to the gods, on the third Friday in October. After the *anaya*, festivities stop. They resume the next month. A memorial service is conducted for those who have died, and a purification rite is performed to rid the village of evil influences. During the celebration, a purification bundle, which includes a shoot of oil palm, a bush rope, and branches of the atizdize tree, is prepared. In the evening the bundle is carried in a procession and buried with prayers that no evil will cross it. Farmers then bring in the new yam crop, and everyone tastes the fruits of the harvest.

For the Abron people the yam festival is also a time to commemorate their arrival in Côte d'Ivoire from the east. The event is lavish with the enthroned king presiding over the festivities. He is dressed in a richly embroidered toga, wears a gold tiara, and holds in his right hand a solid gold scepter. He is covered by a huge scarlet canopy. Around him are his subjects in bright costumes, sitting under colorful umbrellas.

To celebrate the yam festival, Kulango parents and children exchange gifts and eat a meal of mashed yams and soup. Dances and singing are part of the celebrations.

SECULAR HOLIDAYS

NATIONAL DAY, held on December 7, commemorates the country's independence. Ivorians celebrate this happy occasion with traditional processions, dances, and music. Celebrations are held throughout the country, but the biggest is in Yamoussoukro, the city where Félix Houphouët-Boigny was born. On this day, the Guests Palace, an official residence for the president's guests, and City Hall are ablaze with many lights. Thousands attend the grand parade in Yamoussoukro.

NEW YEAR'S DAY is a time to celebrate the renewal of the natural order. It is also a time when all the ethnic groups hold masquerade parties. An important mask used in the celebrations is the plankmask, or *bedu* ("BER-dew"), which represents a wild animal that has been tamed by the mask.

For some people, other crops may be just as important. For example, the Dan people rely heavily on rice as a staple. If the rice harvest is good, young Dan girls will perform a dance as homage to the spirits protecting the crops.

The national dance troupe performing during National Day celebrations.

113

FOOD

FOOD IS A FASCINATING aspect of Ivorian culture. Many dishes are spicy but there are plenty that are mild too. The best eating places are at someone's home or at the food stalls on street corners.

EATING STYLES

In the Ivorian society, eating is not simply a matter of sustaining the body but an expression of the community spirit. The tradition is for all the people in a village to eat together in a common area. The villagers are divided into three groups—women and girls eat as one group, men as another, and young boys as the third. Food is served in large containers and placed on mats on the ground. There is no need for utensils, as the Ivorians use their clean hands to scoop up food instead of a knife and fork. Usually a handful of rice is taken and formed into a ball along with the meat and sauce. After the meal, a wash basin is passed around.

ETIQUETTE

During a meal, the men, women, and children will sit together in their respective groups and eat from a common bowl. It is customary for the elders in the group to start eating first, so that they can detect any poison or contamination in the food. If the food is contaminated, the young are stopped from eating it. It is bad manners to reach across the table to take food because the person would be deemed as greedy.

This practice also ensures that everyone eating from the communal bowl gets a fair share of the food. Coughing or sneezing or anything other than eating at the dinner table is taboo. If one needs to cough, one would get up first and move away from the table. Talking while eating is also discouraged. Whatever needs to be said can be done after the meal. The Ivorians also believe in taking one's time to digest the food.

The right hand is used for making the ball of food because of the long-standing practice of using the left hand to wash.

Opposite: **A woman prepares for a meal by washing the cooking equipment first.**

115

Ivorian staples on sale.

FAVORITE FOODS

Chicken and fish are the favorite foods of Ivorians. However, for many, eating meat is restricted by its high cost and inaccessibility. Thus, vegetables make up a large portion of an Ivorian's diet and provide for significant amounts of vitamins. A typical meal includes staples, such as rice or cassava, and a sauce in which to dip the rice. Leafy vegetables, root crops, and hot peppers are commonly boiled or added to soups and stews. Ivorians do not typically eat dessert, but sometimes fresh fruit is eaten after a meal.

HOT PEPPERS originated in South America. Today they are a staple in Côte d'Ivoire where several varieties are cultivated for local use. There are many kinds of hot peppers of interesting colors and shapes and with varying degrees of hotness. *Habanero* ("HAB-er-near-row"), a type of hot pepper, is more widely cultivated than any other variety and is one of the hottest. The fruit of the *habanero* has a smoky flavor and is usually red or yellow. Ivorians use *habanero* to spice up virtually every dish on the table, because its smoky aroma adds a special taste to soups, stews, and sauces.

YAMS are widely cultivated in Côte d'Ivoire. Both the leaves and the root are eaten. The leaves are steamed and cooked in palm oil with okra, lima beans, hot peppers, and smoked fish, and usually served with rice. The roots may be peeled and boiled or used to make French fries. Yams can range in color from yellow to orange-red to purple, and can be classified into two types—dry or moist. Dry yams have a powdery texture after cooking. Yams are often added to onions and tomatoes and sautéed with peppers. The mixture is boiled until the yams are soft.

IVORIAN CULINARY DELIGHTS

Aloco ("AL-oh-ko") is ripe bananas cooked in palm oil and garnished with steamed onions and chilis. It can be eaten alone or with grilled fish.

Attiéké ("AT-tee-eck-ee") is a popular side dish of grated cassava. *Attiéké* is like couscous, a dish of wheat grain steamed over broth with meat or fruit added, prevalent in many parts of Africa. In Côte d'Ivoire, it is made with cassava.

Kedjenou ("KED-gen-ooh") is chicken cooked with different kinds of vegetables in a mild sauce and wrapped in banana leaves. This dish can be served with yams, *attiéké*, or rice.

N'voufou ("FOO-fue") is mashed bananas or yams mixed with palm oil and served with eggplant sauce.

Foutou ("FOO-too") is made by boiling cassava and bananas until they are cooked. The cassava and banana are then separately pounded with drops of water added from time to time to keep them from sticking and to make them the right consistency. Then both the cassava and banana are mixed together and pounded again. A little salt can be added for additional taste.

CASSAVA, also known as tapioca, is divided into sweet and bitter types. Ivorians enjoy the cassava as a daily staple like rice because it is nutritious and grows easily under a variety of conditions. Both the roots and leaves are edible. Cooking the cassava can be an arduous task because the root contains cyanide, a potentially poisonous salt. It is only after grating, squeezing out the liquid, and cooking that the cassava is safe to eat.

OKRA is another widely grown plant. A typical okra can grow up to 6 feet (1.8 m) tall. The leaves are lobed and are generally hairy. The plant produces dark yellow flowers and then produces pods, which are the edible portion of the plant. Young pods are thinly sliced to prepare okra soup. Tough and fibrous pods are dried and then ground into a powder, which is used for thickening stews. Fresh young pods can be dried for use in soups.

EGGPLANT has erect or spreading branches bearing white or purple fruit. It is cooked and eaten in the same way as other vegetables.

Cassava is a shrubby, tropical, perennial plant introduced by Portuguese sailors from Brazil in the 16th century.

BEVERAGES

Ivorians enjoy drinking ginger beer. It is made with a lot of ginger, almost enough to burn the throat. To make ginger beer, 12 pieces of beaten ginger and an unpeeled pineapple are added to about two quarts of boiling water. The mixture is left to stand overnight. The next day, it is drained, sugar is added, and the drink is chilled. Although not many Ivorians drink beer, except those along the coast, there is a good local brew called Flag. A homemade brew is *bangui* ("BAN-kee"), a local white palm wine. Yeast is added to the juice tapped from the palm tree, and the brew is left to ferment overnight. Apart from beer, soft drinks are the most popular beverages among women who do not drink alcohol.

After a hard day's work, drinking a glass of beer at a *marquis* ("MA-kee") is a good way to relax.

The outdoor market is where most people buy their food. The sellers, mostly women, spread out their produce and wares in large basins. The larger towns and cities will have a few supermarkets, but buying groceries at these places can be expensive.

POPULAR EATING SPOTS

The cities have many restaurants, and Abidjan in particular has several eating places serving French, Italian, Caribbean, Lebanese, and Vietnamese food. A growing trend are establishments catering to non-Africans who want to sample local traditional food. Among them, the *maquis* restaurant is the most popular. It is an inexpensive, outdoor restaurant with chairs and tables or wooden benches and sometimes a sandy floor. It is found almost everywhere throughout the country. Popular dishes in a *maquis* include braised chicken or fish with onions and tomatoes, *attiéké*, and *kedjenou*. To be considered a *maquis*, braised food must be available. A *maquis* usually only opens in the evenings.

At lunchtime in the cities, waitresses set up stands outside restaurants to serve rice or *foutou* with various sauces. Patrons make their choice from delicacies such as fish sauce or gumbo sauce, and then go inside to eat. This service is especially useful for the busy urbanites who drop by for a quick lunch.

ARACHID SAUCE

2 tablespoons peanut butter
water
4 pimentos
18 mashed, baby tomatoes
meat (beef, chicken, or fish)
a pinch of salt
oil
1/2 egg-sized onion

Place the peanut butter in a pot and add twice the amount of water. Mix well until it is sauce-like and add another cup of water. Bring the sauce to a hard boil and add two more cups of water over a 25-minute period. Add the pimentos. Take 12 baby tomatoes, remove the seeds, and mash. Add the tomato mash and another four cups of water to the sauce and continue to boil. After 50 minutes of boiling, add 2 1/2 more cups of water, then let it boil again gently for 20 minutes. Add precooked meat of choice and a pinch of salt and keep boiling for an additional 35 minutes. Add six more baby tomatoes, prepared as before, a tablespoon of oil, and the mashed onion. Cook for at least another 15 minutes.

KEDJENOU

Traditionally the *kedjenou* is slow-cooked in a large earthenware jar with a narrow neck, which is placed directly over the wood fire. If it is being cooked out in the bush, the food is secured in a banana leaf and placed under the ashes.

3 1/2 lbs (1 1/2 kg) chicken
1 eggplant, cut into small pieces
2 large onions, finely chopped
2 fresh red or green hot peppers, seeded and cut into shreds
4 tomatoes, peeled, seeded, and finely crushed
1 small piece of ginger root, grated
1 sprig thyme and 1 bay leaf
salt

Clean the chicken and cut into pieces. Place in the earthenware jar with the eggplant, onions, peppers, tomatoes, ginger root, thyme, bay leaf, and salt. Hermetically seal the jar by tying a banana leaf around the collar so that air does not escape. No water needs to be added during cooking. Place the jar on the hot coals and cook for about 45 minutes. During cooking, raise the jar and shake it vigorously occasionally so that the food does not stick to the bottom.

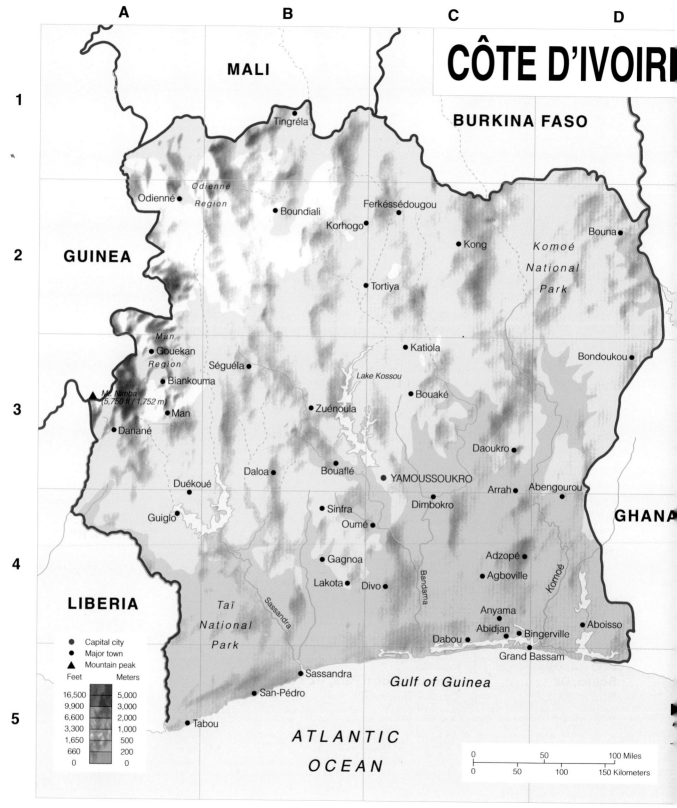

CÔTE D'IVOIRE

MALI

BURKINA FASO

Tingréla

Odienné
Odienné Region

Boundiali

Ferkéssédougou

Korhogo

GUINEA

Kong

Komoé National Park

Bouna

Tortiya

Man Region
Gouekan

Séguéla

Katiola

Bondoukou

Biankouma

Lake Kossou

▲ Mt. Nimba
(5,750 ft / 1,752 m)

Man

Zuénoula

Bouaké

Danané

Daoukro

Daloa

Bouaflé

● YAMOUSSOUKRO

Arrah

Abengourou

Duékoué

Sinfra

Dimbokro

GHANA

Guiglo

Oumé

Adzopé

LIBERIA

Gagnoa

Agboville

Lakota

Divo

Bandama

Komoé

Taï National Park

Sassandra

Anyama

Dabou

Abidjan

Bingerville

Aboisso

Grand Bassam

● Capital city
● Major town
▲ Mountain peak

Sassandra

San-Pédro

Gulf of Guinea

Tabou

Feet	Meters
16,500	5,000
9,900	3,000
6,600	2,000
3,300	1,000
1,650	500
660	200
0	0

ATLANTIC

OCEAN

0   50   100 Miles

0   50   100   150 Kilometers

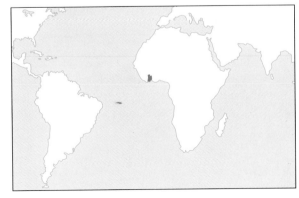

QUICK NOTES

OFFICIAL NAME
République de Côte d'Ivoire

FORMER NAME
Ivory Coast

DATE OF INDEPENDENCE
August 7, 1960

NATIONAL FLAG
Three equal vertical bands of orange (hoist side), white, and green. Design based on the flag of France.

LAND AREA
124,470 square miles (322,460 sq km)

COASTLINE
320 miles (515 km)

MAIN RIVERS
Sassandra, Bandama, Komoé

CLIMATE
Tropical along coast, semiarid in far north

HIGHEST POINT
Mount Nimba (5,750 feet / 1,752 m)

CAPITAL
Yamoussoukro

MAIN CITIES
Abidjan, Bouaké, Man, Korhogo, Bondoukou, San-Pédro

PORTS AND HARBORS
Abidjan, Aboisso, Dabou, San-Pédro

POPULATION
14,986,218 (July 1997)

CURRENCY
African Financial Community franc (CFA)
US$1 = 606.66 CFA francs (1998)

MAIN EXPORTS
Cocoa, coffee, tropical woods, cotton, bananas, petroleum, pineapples, palm oil

MAIN IMPORTS
Food, consumer goods, capital goods, fuel, transportation equipment

MAJOR LANGUAGES
French (official language), Dioula, Senufo, Agni, Baule, Dan/Yacouba

MAJOR ETHNIC GROUPS
Baule (23%)
Senufo (15%)
Agni (11%)

MAJOR RELIGIONS
Indigenous religions (65%)
Islam (23%)
Christianity (12%)

POLITICAL LEADERS
Félix Houphouët-Boigny
President Henri Konan-Bédié
Prime Minister Daniel Kablan Duncan

GLOSSARY

anaya ("a-NAI-ya")
Offering of food to the gods during the yam festival.

attiéké ("AT-tee-eck-ee")
Grated cassava dish.

awale ("a-WA-lay")
Ivorian game similar to backgammon.

bedu ("BER-dew")
Plankmask used in New Year's Day celebrations.

Eid al-Adha
Feast of the sacrifice that marks the end of the pilgrimage to Mecca.

Eid al-Fitr
Celebration of the breaking of the fast at the end of the Islamic month of Ramadan.

Fête des Masques
Festival of masks celebrated annually by the Dan people.

Fête du Dipri
Feast of Dipri celebrated by the Abidji.

gendarmerie ("SHON-dar-mer-ee")
Branch of armed forces responsible for general law enforcement.

griot ("GREE-oh")
People who play praise-sing, keep oral histories, and recite family lineages.

grisgris ("GREE-gree")
Charmed necklaces believed to ward off evil.

Hadith
Collection of Prophet Mohammed's sayings that supplements the Koran in guiding Muslims.

hajj ("HAHJ")
Muslim pilgrimage to Mecca.

kedjenou ("KED-gen-ooh")
Chicken cooked with many kinds of vegetables.

kora ("KOH-rah")
A 21-string musical instrument that is a cross between a harp and a lute.

Koran
Holy book of Islam.

marabous ("MAR-e-boo")
Traditional religious leaders.

marquis ("MA-kee")
Outdoor eating place.

PDCI
Democratic Party of Côte d'Ivoire, the leading political party in the country.

salat ("sa-LAHT")
Muslim prayer.

SAVAC
Special Anti-Crime Police Brigade.

surete ("SUR-eh-tay")
National police.

zakat ("za-KAHT")
Muslim practice of giving alms.

BIBLIOGRAPHY

Côte d'Ivoire In Pictures. Minneapolis: Lerner Publications Company, 1988.

Gottlieb, Alma & Graham, Phillip. *Parallel Worlds.* New York: Crown Publishing, 1993.

Krummer, Patricia K. *Côte d'Ivoire, Enchantment of the World.* Children's Press, 1996.

Sandler, Bea. *The African Cookbook.* New York: Carol Publishing Group, 1993.

INDEX

INDEX

INDEX